T0370199

EVERYTHING I LEARNED ABOUT STOCK INVESTING

ACROSS THE STREET FROM WALL ST

DAVE GRETTA

Author of *Night Trading*

Across The Street From Wall Street
Everything I Learned About Stock Investing

© 2024 Dave Gretta

Print ISBN: 979-8-35097-662-5

DISCLAIMER

This publication is presented solely for educational and informational purposes. If you wish to apply the ideas and concepts contained herein, you do so at your own risk. This publication is intended to provide accurate and authoritative information with regard to the subject matter covered as available at the time of publication; however, they are provided without representation or warranties with respect to the accuracy or completeness of its contents, and the author and publisher specifically disclaim any implied warranties of merchantability or fitness for a particular purpose. This publication is sold with the understanding that the author and publisher are not rendering legal, accounting, financial, or other professional service. Each company, trader, and transaction are different, and the advice and strategies contained herein might not be suitable to your situation. The services of a competent professional should be sought where appropriate. The author and publisher specifically disclaim any liability, loss, or risk, personal or otherwise, incurred as a consequence, directly or indirectly, of the use and application of any of the contents of this publication. In addition, one or more of the investment securities discussed in this publication may have been held, may currently be held, and/or may be held in the future by the author, and nothing in this publication should be considered a recommendation to buy or sell any such investment security. The information and content written and/or disseminated by

CONTENTS

INTRODUCTION
SHOCKED

A Michelin star rating is one of the most prestigious honors a restaurant can receive. The highest Michelin rating is 3 stars, and defined as "exceptional cuisine." If I asked you to cook a really good dinner, would you be able to? Cooking is not as easy as it looks, and most people, and restaurants, are not expert at cooking 3-star Michelin meals. That's ok, most people are not great at picking stocks and stock investing either. I've learned this harsh truth from what I've observed throughout my life, and since I wrote and published my last stock investing book *Night Trading*. Just like many stock investing books, cookbooks give you recipes with a very defined set of steps to follow. You just need to follow the instructions. Sounds simple. But many, including myself, often manage to bungle cooking. I suspect most of us would be happy if we could just cook a one- star Michelin meal, the lowest rating, which denotes "very good." Interestingly enough, the iconic Michelin rating is named after a French tire company.

Stock investing is something where you can seemingly do everything correct, according to the 'recipe,' yet still manage to lose money or underperform the S&P 500 Index. Legendary stock investor Charlie Munger said one of the most important lessons investors can learn is that 99% of stock investing involves doing nothing. It seems many people are perceived as or consider themselves lazy. If true, then shouldn't most people be great stock investors? Sadly, the answer is no.

You would think most people could master something as simple as falling asleep at night. But, according to the Centers for Disease Control and Prevention, about 1 in 3 adults in the United States reports not getting enough rest or sleep every day. Also, an estimated 50 to 70 million Americans have chronic, or ongoing, sleep disorders, according to recent government estimates. How then, is the average person going to be a successful stock investor if they can't master everyday things like cooking and sleeping? Keep in mind, cooking and sleeping are what many consider two relatively simple tasks in life. Achieving long-term success in stock investing is not easy.

I have traveled across the United States and spoken to many stock investors (and non-investors). In speaking with a bunch of college educated 20-somethings I know, none of them could even find Antarctica on a map when I asked them to find it. Not surprisingly, none of them knew much of anything about stock investing either when I questioned them about it. Once, two forty-year-olds I met told me they never invested in a single stock their entire lives, and further told me they don't even know how to buy a stock. One woman I came across worked on Wall Street during the Great Financial Crisis in 2008, and lost $18 million in a two-week span because her investments were not diversified. She had almost her entire net worth in what ended up being worthless company bank stock.

My doctor makes hundreds of thousands of dollars a year, but told me they don't understand stock investing so they "don't really invest much." One night my neighbor showed me his Robinhood account balance and how much money he lost. It was a fairly substantial amount, given that he was only in his twenties. I was stunned for two reasons. First, it was 2023 and the stock market was mostly up that year, and, in fact, ended up having one of its best years ever. Second, he had bought my first stock investing book *Night Trading* (the entire book is only 100 pages by the way) in 2022. The problem, he told me, was that he was so busy, he never got around to reading my book.

Sadly, even my own family members are not excluded from doing 'dumb things' regarding stock investing. I spend a chapter in this book discussing my own aunt who left a million dollars on the table in the stock market.

We are told to listen to the financial and stock advice of the 'experts' on popular financial news networks. Should we have listened to the 'expert' I found that regularly appears on the cable news networks, but publicly apologized in a video put out in early 2024 that they were "astonishingly wrong" about their stock picks and advice for the entire year of 2023? Remember, 2023 was also a year the stock market saw huge gains. Seems like we need Yelp for stock analysts.

Tom Brady won seven National Football League Super Bowl titles, is a multi-millionaire, and seems like a very smart guy. So, should we listen to him for stock advice? Brady was a very public investor and spokesperson for the publicly traded companies Wheels Up, Hertz, and failed crypto exchange FTX. Has anyone checked how these three investments are doing today? Not great, as some are not even in business anymore. Speaking of celebrities, maybe we should listen to the stock advice of Taylor Swift, if she gave any. She seems to have managed her money extremely well. For decades her dad worked as a financial advisor for wealth management firm The Swift Group, which operated under investment management firm Merrill Lynch. So, maybe I would personally listen to Taylor Swift's stock advice.

I feel like a comedian that is constantly getting new material for a standup comedy show. Maybe I should go on tour with famous comedian Bill Burr. All joking aside, investing your hard-earned money is no laughing matter. In my travels and talks around the country, I discovered three alarming things, which motivated me to write this stock investing book:

1. Many people do not invest in stocks at all.

2. Many invest in stocks and lose money.

3. Some invested in stocks and made lots of money, but then lost most of it investing again, likely because of ego and poor judgement. Remember, even Albert Einstein eventually lost most of his money in the 1929 stock market crash, and look how smart he was.

I found a few of these people on Financial Twitter (also called FinTwit and now we might call it FinX). Someone professed on YouTube they made around $4 million in stock investing over the course of several years, and then lost $3 million of it in the bear stock market of 2022. Weirdly, they admitted all this on their own YouTube videos, for the entire world to see. Another person admitted in a long interview on Financial YouTube that they lost $485,000 in a single day trading one stock. Another person I know lost well into five figures investing in metaverse real estate, which is almost worthless now. I could go on, but it is too depressing quite frankly. There are a few high-profile accounts on Financial Twitter and Financial YouTube I'd love to go out for a beer with; but taking investing advice from not so much. From my experience and observations, I would not confuse some of the high-profile stock investing influencers you see on Financial Twitter or Financial YouTube with someone you'd see sitting at a blackjack table in Atlantic City or Las Vegas at 2am in the morning; they may in fact be the same person. Or, at the very least, share many of the same traits.

A search on Amazon for 'stock investing books' returns about 40,000 books. In my opinion, a great deal of these books might not be very good or useful, based on the sampling I have read throughout my life. Actually, if you don't believe me, there is a video interview out there on YouTube with one of the top-selling stock investing book authors in history, who said he'd donate most of the stock investing books he's read to a yard sale. The fact that there are so many tens of thousands of stock investing books, tells me the stock market may not be as 'efficient' as many would argue. The *Efficient Markets Hypothesis* states that share prices reflect all information. Yeah right. If having success in stock investing was so easy, as some apparently think, then why are there so many stock investing books? Many stock investing books are redundant, in my opinion, and may not be relevant to your investing situation or time horizon. You may have read a few stock investing books where half the book is good, but not the other half. I know I have. Some are too long, just plain confusing, or honestly just too damn boring. If your plan in life is to read one hundred stock investing books that is great, but I would argue it will take a long time, and you could easily get yourself distracted and confused by reading so many. Malcolm Gladwell famously said, "There can be as much value in the blink of an eye as in months of rational analysis." So, it seems, do not bury your head too long in stock investing books, because things may not play out in real life exactly like they are written.

I think the way to approach stock investing is to first sit back and take a deep breath and figure out how you 'look at and think about' the stock market. I can tell you from first-hand experience this is not easy. I come from an accounting background and I got an 'A' in the Intermediate Accounting course at the very popular business graduate school I attended just a few blocks from Wall Street. Many things regarding stock investing, and even audited financial statements, are 'subject to interpretation.' This can make things very cloudy when trying to analyze stocks.

Regarding technical stock analysis and interpreting stock charts, everyone can interpret a chart differently; for example, is it a double top or cup-with-handle? Stock investing involves making many decisions and, just like anything in life, every decision can lead to failure. In my opinion, stock investing involves three main decisions: picking a stock to buy, finding the 'right price' to buy the stock, and when to sell the stock. None of these three decisions are easy.

I don't want the stock market to consume my life. I just want to leverage the stock market to my advantage so I can make some money. The below pie chart is a simple illustration of where stock investing fits in my life.

Your Life

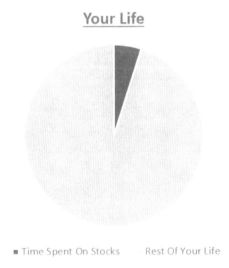

■ Time Spent On Stocks   Rest Of Your Life

I have no desire to make the tiny 'time spent on stocks' section any bigger in my life. It would be as if someone walked up to me and said: Do you want to be a fulltime professional gambler or blackjack player? Many equate stock investing and trading to gambling, and I doubt most people would want to be a full-time professional poker player.

I detest when people say investing success just takes time. While it may be partly true, the statement is made under the assumption you have a lot of time. But what if you don't have a lot of time? What if you were a 60-year-old stock investor and sold your entire stock portfolio when Covid hit in 2020 when the stock market briefly crashed? What if you didn't get back into the stock market, and subsequently missed its massive runup soon after government stimulus? Or, what if you get divorced and end up losing half your money? According to current data, there is about a 50% chance of that happening if you are currently married. Or maybe you feel you can never start investing because you have a massive amount of student loans from college to payoff. Or, you may have gotten yourself into colossal credit card debt that you need to eliminate first. Sadly, some never really get off the ground in their investing journey.

There is no 'right way' to invest, but I'm sure there are many wrong ways. There is no shortage of stock advice out there; it is well-intentioned, but it can be dangerous to use someone else's map of reality to navigate yours, even if they are experienced. Learn to filter and selectively implement advice. Often, it might be best to tune out everyone's stock advice and listen to what the stock is saying, specifically the stock's price. We spend an entire chapter analyzing and interpreting stock charts.

I have a theory that the same people that do badly in the stock market also listen to the mechanic at the oil change place to change their oil *exactly* every 3,000 miles. They even give you a sticker to put on your windshield to remind you to come back soon, so you can spend more money on their oil change services. There is a parallel from this oil change logic to stock investing. That same type of 'oil change' thinking is too logical and normal, as is the fact many think stock investing success also involves normal and logical thinking. As you will soon find out in this book, the stock market is mostly not a normal and logical place. In fact, the opposite of what the masses think often happens in the stock market.

Anyone who drives a gas-powered car is likely to have heard you must change your engine oil every 3,000 miles. That is a myth. Changing your oil every 3,000 miles will not hurt your engine. It just won't likely help it either, and if you asked ten people what mileage you should change your motor oil, you'd likely get ten different answers. The same might happen if you ask ten people their thoughts on a particular stock. The oil change dilemma becomes even more complex when you introduce synthetic motor oil into the discussion. By the way, I never listen to the oil change mechanic. I always go at least 5,000 miles between oil changes on regular oil. Sometimes, I even get crazy and go much longer than 5,000 miles. By the way, if you own an electric vehicle, you never have to worry about oil changes.

The stock market is the great equalizer; it can make smart people look stupid and stupid people look smart. A book only needs one good idea to make it a worthwhile investment. This book, I am positive, has many great teachings and investing ideas. Just zoom out and think; even if you analyzed stocks 24/7/365 you might still fail at it. That's what professional money managers on Wall Street do, and it's reported that at least 80% of them can't beat the S&P 500 Index returns over time.

The title of this book comes from my experiences working at One Liberty Plaza, a skyscraper in the Financial District of Lower Manhattan in New York City, for a large part of my twenties. This is the tall, black building right across the street from the former Twin Towers at the World Trade Center. The building was discussed on the news in the September 2001 attacks on the Trade Center, and was said to be leaning that day. One Liberty Plaza was reported to be near collapse, but was later found to have no structural damage and only some broken glass. While working there, I could look out my office window thirty-five floors up and see the New York Stock Exchange. I learned a lot about stocks, investing, and life working in lower Manhattan, and attending graduate school in the few blocks surrounding the New York Stock Exchange. This book contains fundamental stock analysis, some technical stock analysis with charts, and a lot of mental approaches to both stock investing and life. I garnered most of what I know about the stock market and how the stock market works from people that were already highly successful in playing this game. I wrote this book to try to download everything that I learned being at the center of the stock investing universe, right to your brain.

Investing in stocks is something that should be appealing to everyone, regardless of what you do for a living. No matter what you do in life, you should be investing something. "Investing puts money to work. The only reason to save money is to invest it," says well-known real estate investor and bestselling author Grant Cardone. The problem with stock investing is that a lot of things must work in your favor for you to actually make money in the stock market, which is why so many people are scared of investing. Why, you might ask, would some fear the stock market, something that statistically about 3 out of every 4 years goes up and over long periods of time goes up pretty appreciably? The answer is simple: If, for example, you went out to the casino with your friends one night and lost all your money gambling, you likely wouldn't go back to the casino again for a very long time. Some might never go back.

Risk is always a factor in stock investing, and we will discuss risk in detail. You must ask yourself what method of transportation you want to take getting from Point A to Point B in your stock investing journey. Do you want to ride a motorcycle or drive a car? Both can get you to the destination, but one method is far safer and less risky than the other. So, get in your car now, put on your seatbelt, lock the doors, and come along for the ride.

CHAPTER 1

BIG PICTURE – DEVELOP YOUR GAME PLAN

Y ou've probably read other stock investing books before. Or, maybe this is your first. Either way, before we get started with this book, I suggest you read a book about money that I have prior read. I am sure you never started reading a book where the author suggests you stop reading their book and read another book first. It's important to get your mind right, and how you think about money, *before* you invest. If you don't like money, it's doubtful money will ever be attracted to you. Therefore, I recommend you read a book that I have read several times: *Money Grows On Trees.* As the subtitle of the book states, it will teach you how to reshape your thoughts, beliefs, and ideals about money. This 140-page paperback book is available on Amazon, and last time I checked was selling for under ten dollars. It's an easy read too. Some of us may have misconceptions about money that were, for better or worse, instilled in us at a young age from our parents and grandparents. The book goes over all this, and points your mind in the right direction regarding money. It's filled with inspiring stories and, in my opinion, should be a required read for everyone and anyone age twenty and up. Take note that I will not be referring to the *Trees* book at all in this book, it's just a financial mindset book I'd highly recommend you read.

OK. Welcome back. Now we can get started with my newest stock investing book here. One piece of advice before getting started is that I highly recommend reading A*cross The Street* (hereafter I will refer to this book with this shortened title) in chapter order, as this is a book that will just flow better if you read it in chapter order, as each chapter cumulatively builds on concepts of prior chapters.

The Story Behind *Night Trading*

I want to point something out regarding my last stock investing book; **Night Trading: How To Learn And Invest In The Stock Market…At Night.** No need to worry if you did not read it, because most of that entire book is woven into this book. You're essentially getting two books in one here. If you did not read my last book **Night Trading**, here is a brief synopsis of that book.

night trading

noun

1 the opposite of day trading

2 the practice of researching, buying, and selling stocks at night to make a profit

What do day trading and night trading have in common? Not much, but we will learn how having the mindset of both can be helpful to your overall investing. *Night Trading* takes some of what I observed from these two divergent investor ideas, and synthesizes it with my vast investing knowledge and experience to try to create long-term wealth.

Night Trading is for the beginning and sophisticated investor. *Night Trading*, along with this book, is also a primer to educate high school and college students in financial literacy and investing. You will learn time-tested investment methods, sprinkled in with new investment trends like Bitcoin. Other creative investment ideas and approaches will enable you to leverage all the free investment information out there and use it to your advantage. You will learn to invest 'outside the box' to take calculated risks, while being grounded in proven investment methods.

It is impossible to get lucky consistently in the stock market, so you have to know what you're doing. When investing in the stock market, knowledge is power, and you need to arm yourself with information. I am shocked most of the wealthy people that I know do not understand the stock market or investing in it at all. If you have enough money and want to buy stocks then you must diversify, which also means you should read this book to understand what you're doing.

The idea behind night trading, and my book *Night Trading*, is that there is no need to quit your day job to achieve financial success in stock investing. I have learned from 'the best of the best' in finance and investing, and am passing on that knowledge to you in this book.

I bought my first stock when I was a junior in high school. Growing up in the New Jersey suburbs just outside of Manhattan, I was about a one-hour bus ride from Wall Street. I remember watching the movie *Wall Street* and reading books about Wall Street tycoons, like Peter Lynch, and other high profile stock market investors. I was hooked. I dreamed of one day visiting Wall Street, and since I lived so close, I figured this would happen eventually. I didn't know how or when I would get to Wall Street, but I was positive I would get there.

One day, while I was still in high school, I received a letter in the mail from the company in which I owned stock. Granted, I think I only owned ten shares, but you have to start somewhere. The letter invited me to the annual shareholders meeting in Manhattan, located in an office building just one block from the New York Stock Exchange. Back then, before Zoom and video meetings over the internet, most shareholder meetings were 'in person' gatherings. At only age seventeen, I had finally punched my ticket to Wall Street, and I had goose bumps. However, the shareholder meeting was on a week-day, a school day. So, I did what any teenager in high school would do; I skipped school. Picture the comedy movie *Ferris Bueller's Day Off*. *Ferris Bueller's Day Off* tells the story of a high school student, Ferris, who skips school with his best friend and his girlfriend Sloane for a day in Chicago. Luckily, the bus station to Manhattan was less than a two-mile drive from my high school. My dream culminated when I took a bus to lower Manhattan to check out Wall Street and the metal Wall Street bull, located just a few blocks from the New York Stock Exchange. By the way, that metal bull is made of bronze.

I remember arriving at the front desk of the building for the shareholders meeting and a building security guard saying to me; "Who the hell are you?" I was tall and skinny at the time, probably only weighing 125 pounds, and wearing glasses. They probably figured I should be in school. I answered: "I'm Dave Gretta and I'm here for the annual shareholders' meeting." They showed me to the elevator, and off I went to the meeting.

My career goal as a child was to become a stockbroker. What's funny today, as investors become increasingly autonomous, you rarely hear anyone say they want to be a stockbroker. I don't even think they're called stockbrokers anymore. They are mostly called financial advisors or financial planners now. With the advent of commission-free stock trades on platforms like Robinhood, E*TRADE, Fidelity, and many others, you really don't need a stockbroker to purchase stocks anymore, and you can research stocks for free. I try to spend some time each night watching the financial news and researching stocks. I do all this while holding down a fulltime "day job" in information technology. I consider myself an eclectic investor, who is well-connected to professional investors that do this for a living. I hold an MBA in Financial Management. I have invested and traded since I was a teenager. I previously worked in Accounting and Finance at a billion-dollar international insurance company literally *across the street* from Wall Street, so I am also well versed in preparing financial statements and analyzing financial data.

My life has now come full circle. I have two teenagers in high school, and I volunteer some time guest teaching a class at their high school called <u>Basic Stock Market Investing</u>. I like to start the class by saying that investing in stocks is extremely complex, and if you don't know what you're doing you will eventually lose all or most of your money. I believe we need to teach financial literacy not only to our high school students, but people at most every age after high school.

Would you ever try to play a musical instrument like the piano or electric guitar without taking lessons? No. It is the same thing with the stock market, and buying and selling stocks. You shouldn't invest without studying and learning the stock market; let alone spend, and potentially lose, your hard-earned money. Theoretically, a stock cannot go below zero, so at worst you could potentially just lose your initial investment, but I'm not sure that is a comforting thought. The good news, is you don't even have to attend college or receive formalized training to achieve success in the stock market. But you do need to know what you are doing.

I also coach my kids' youth basketball teams. I always preach that when shooting the basketball, it's not shooting - it's aiming. Same thing with stocks – you cannot just use a 'shotgun' approach and invest scattershot without knowledge or a plan. It's true, some investors might get lucky a few times, but remember, a broken clock is still right twice a day. Your investment strategy should mentally be more like aiming a basketball – not shooting a basketball. You have to aim and think about the ball going through the basket. With stock investing, the aiming is the free investment research you need to be doing, and the intelligent processing of that information.

You may have to forget about some of the traditional metrics that you were taught to value stocks, because they may not work in today's investment world. There are many more technology companies today, and they have things called intangible assets and goodwill that make it extremely difficult for anyone to accurately value them. Even the so-called stock market 'experts' may not know what these companies are worth. **Across The Street** devotes two entire chapters discussing this and helping you figure it out.

Most things I do in life I always ask myself the question: Why? Why am I thinking about doing whatever it is I am considering at the time? Why do I want to buy a car? Should I lease a car instead of buying one? So, why do you want to invest in the stock market? Everyone needs to ask themselves and answer this important question. The main reason I invest in individual stocks is to have control of what I own. I often try to buy into companies whose product I use and enjoy, or I know somebody that works at the company. Quite a few of the stocks I own I do have a connection to – either I work with or use their product, or I know someone that uses their product.

Or, I know someone that knows someone that uses their product. You get the idea.

You may be asking - what was the genesis behind my first book *Night Trading*? A culmination of a lifetime of formal schooling in finance and studying the greats like Buffett, Lynch, and Bogle for hundreds of hours. I spent extensive time pouring through and studying the latest finance and investment articles. This 'hunker down' investment mentality was further exacerbated by the global pandemic in March 2020. After all, there was not much to do for a year when the world was basically in lockdown from the global pandemic; so, why not write a book. Writing a book about the stock market, and sharing my unique experiences on Wall Street, had always been an idea in the back of my mind anyway.

What is the definition of night trading? I have met some fulltime day traders and I can say I have NO interest in ever becoming a day trader. I do share one commonality with day traders, and that is a love of investing in stocks, just in a different way. I work a fulltime day job in information technology; therefore, I do all my stock investing research and stock purchases and sales at night – often late into the night. So, one day I was joking around with my friends and I said what I do is *Night Trading*. I like to invest for the long term. I also thought the term night trading would resonate well with people and as a book title. The term 'day trading' is already ingrained in most people's minds, so I just thought why not *Night Trading* as the name of my first book. I have another good friend that works for one of the largest banks in the world. He only invests in solid, dividend paying companies for the long term. I recently asked him when was the last time he sold a stock and he said about twenty years ago! He has done extremely well in his stock market investments using a long-term buy and hold strategy. Long-term "buy and hold" is the opposite of day trading. I refer to it as **Night Trading**.

We Now Continue the *Across The Street* Journey

Investing in stocks is my thing. I have many wealthy friends, and barely any of them got wealthy investing *just* in stocks. Most of their wealth came from owning their own business and investing in real estate. Does this tell you something?

If you have real estate tenants, it brings in monthly income and provides a great tax write-off. Have you noticed that most people that own real estate don't pay a lot of taxes? And have you ever noticed that most Hollywood actors and actresses, for example, invest heavily in real estate? You never hear what stocks Ben Affleck or Brad Pitt or Jennifer Aniston invest in, but you do read about all the beautiful homes and vacation residences they own. Case in point, a relatively new and upcoming Hollywood star actress, Sydney Sweeney, invests a lot in real estate. She has appeared in some very cool and popular movies, and I have watched most of them. Note that she is only 26 years old. I did an online search of her net worth, and the consensus seems to be around $40 million (note that this number is only an estimate). In addition to acting, Sweeney invests in real estate, buying mansions in Los Angeles and Florida. Online searches indicate she owns roughly five houses, totaling approximately $25 million. You must figure that her $40 million in salary income is heavily taxed. So, after taxes, it is apparent that she has spent a sizeable percentage of her net worth on real estate. One article stated she bought a mansion in Florida for a considerable discount, almost $5 million off the original asking price. I'm sure Hollywood actors and actresses can snag these great deals because they can pay in all cash. The point is that she is clearly investing an extremely large part of her net worth in real estate, not risky stocks. I think that is a smart move for her situation. She likely is investing some in stocks, but that information is not disclosed to the public.

Real estate also appears to be very resilient, because during the pandemic of 2020 it seems real estate was one of the few assets that never really dropped at all. It held its value and actually appreciated, while just about everything else dropped in value before eventually rebounding. Speaking of real estate values rebounding, I should mention one of Brad Pitt's real estate investments. In 2012, Pitt purchased a French winery called Chateau Miraval for an estimated $60 million. Fast forward to 2024, and the winery is worth an estimated $500 million. Not a bad rate of return. Sure, you may have been able to find a stock that did a 10x during that time frame, but I am pretty sure it would likely have been much more difficult to find, and far riskier than real estate.

Real estate takes a lot of manual labor and time to invest in directly if you are flipping houses or renting properties. Further, if you're a younger investor and do not have a lot of capital then it's going to be difficult to invest in real estate. I actually do invest in real estate, but through a real estate investment trust (REIT). REITs are very popular and you might hear people talk about investing in REITs. Keep in mind, though, just because a REIT is 'backed' by real estate, it doesn't necessarily mean it is a risk-free investment. Once you package any investment, REITs included, into a stock that can be traded on an exchange, it automatically becomes risky. Any company's stock is subject to the opinions and emotions of everyone else in the stock market, and those people's opinions regarding what they think your stock is worth change daily.

What attracts me to investing in stocks is that you can do it all while sitting on your sofa, essentially pressing a few buttons on your laptop or cell phone. All the work in stock market investing is done in your brain. Another great appeal of stock investing is that it is a highly liquid investment that you can get quickly in and out of. If you are invested in a bad stock that you don't like you can always sell the stock. Conversely, real estate is not a very liquid investment. If you are in a bad real estate investment, it could take a while to sell your house and unwind your position. Warren Buffett never invested much in real estate. His reasoning is that, under most conditions, it's hard to find mispriced assets in the real estate market. Buffett famously targets assets that are trading at a discount to intrinsic value, and that's not common in the real estate sector.

Across The Street expands on the real estate concept of buying or renting to try to answer the question of which method is better when it comes to stock investing. Is the day trader who 'rents' a stock, or the long-term investor the better way to invest? Or is it somewhere in the middle? Do you need to explore non-traditional ways of investing in equities? Do you need to look at other investments outside of traditional equities altogether, like Bitcoin? This will all be explored, but you need to read this book to find out. People apply this "buy or rent" concept to many things in daily life, like buying or leasing a car or a house, for example. An extreme example of this 'rent everything' philosophy that is pervading the world is a company called Netbricks (https://netbricks.biz) that, believe it or not, rents out LEGOs – those interlocking plastic construction toys.

Across The Street will also prove that traditional fundamental stock analysis can still be applied and remain useful in many instances today. This will be discussed in Chapter 4. That is my favorite chapter, and I feel the price of this book is worth it just for what you can learn in that chapter alone.

I find that financial *illiteracy* also extends into adulthood and often until retirement, unfortunately, for a lot of people. *Across The Street* lays a foundation for students to build strong money habits early on and avoid many of the mistakes that lead to lifelong money struggles. The reality is that many states and school districts do not provide any substantive personal finance education, if they provide any at all. High school seems like the best and most logical place to start delivering personal finance education to America's youth. I have been a part of volunteering my time to teach high school students about stock market investing, and this is outlined in Chapter 27.

You must first ask yourself if investing in the stock market even makes financial sense for you. The stock market has historically returned around 10% per year (before accounting for inflation). While that's a healthy return, it's also significantly lower than the average credit card interest rate of around 22%. For the average consumer, that makes paying off credit card debt an indisputable priority over investing in the stock market. Translation – if you have credit card debt interest of at least 22% or more, then you shouldn't invest in stocks unless you can guarantee you can make more than a 22% return. So, please make sure you have your financial life somewhat in order before starting out on your stock investing journey.

The investment advice in this book is timeless, as it was cultivated over many years by proven finance professionals and it should be helpful throughout your life, so plan on passing this book down to your children. One has to be open-minded to realize that the world is constantly changing, and know there is a need to always sprinkle in new investment ideas. Your ability to adapt will serve you well in investing, and life. This was all covered in my last stock investing book, **Night Trading**. The main point of the name of that book was that you can do all this work at night after you get home from your day job. Or, if you do not work during the day, you can read this book after things settle down for you at night – a testament to the "money never sleeps" quote from the movie *Wall Street.* Another point of **Night Trading** is a play on the term day trading, with emphasis on having a long-term investment strategy.

You can also make money doing some short-term investing as well. A few years ago, I invested a small amount of money in a cryptocurrency coin and made a 130% return in just 72 hours. Don't get me wrong, investing in an S&P 500 Index fund can be a great long-term investment, and I do own one. However, a 100% or 200% return in a short amount of time can be a nice complement to what you could earn in an S&P 500 Index fund over, say, seven years. Seven years is the average time it has historically taken to double your money in an S&P 500 Index fund.

Ideally, you will sit back and develop your own investment thesis and what works for you. Strive to cultivate an investment philosophy that fits what you like to invest in. To use a sports analogy, imagine shooting a foul shot in basketball. You have to filter out all the noise and distractions. People forget that right before shooting a foul shot in basketball, the player was likely running at full speed trying to score - so take a deep breath and get your legs underneath you. There is A LOT of investment information out there in the world. Keep in mind that entire books could be, and have been, written on almost every chapter in this book, thus proving it is very easy to get overwhelmed in the stock market world.

Start by taking a macroeconomic view of the world first. There is a need to look at the 'big picture' investment landscape and ask yourself; why will stocks go up in the near future and the long term? At the time of this writing, we have 'high-ish' interest rates and elevated inflation. The job market and stock market are both doing well, though. Inflation, however, is something that can eventually wreck the stock market, and the economy in general. Inflation will be discussed in greater detail in Chapter 15.

There is also commission-free investing now, which helps everyone get on the on-ramp to the stock market. We also have a healthy IPO environment and I think you will see that there's pent-up demand, that IPOs increase in the future. I also took a look at how much money is going to be pumped into the stock market in the future due to the trillions of dollars that will be passed down in inheritance. Some estimates say as much as many tens of trillions of dollars will be passed down from current Baby Boomers (the generation of people born between 1944 and 1964), the wealthiest generation in American history. A large chunk of this money will likely find its way into the stock market.

I look at people like myself, who enjoy stock investing and want to understand it, as having a similar mindset to people that work at or invest in hedge funds. A hedge fund is a pooled investment fund that manages money for large institutions, high-net worth individuals, and large financial companies, with the goal of achieving alpha returns. An alpha return just means better returns than the broader market. Simply put, hedge funds exist and are offered to try to give people an edge in the market and with their investments. Like hedge funds, I am just trying to maximize my investment returns. The companies that manage hedge funds must do their homework, as do individual investors like ourselves, to try to beat the S&P 500 Index returns. Obviously, I do not advocate allocating a large portion of your money to speculative investments nor do I guarantee that you could achieve large, consistent returns. The first objective of investing, be it in stocks or anything else, is not to lose money.

For myself, I also compare stock investing to other types of investments I could be making, and for me the stock market is the best. Gold is not a bad investment, but just not my 'cup of tea.' I also think gold for years suffered from a $2,000 "hardcap"; meaning it has been historically difficult for it to get to and stay above that price per ounce. Lately, though, with high inflation, it seems to have pierced that magical $2,000 mark and even hit $2,500. It appears that $2,000 is good price support for gold going forward. Gold is considered safe, but some would say it is 'painfully safe.' I am going to 'cherry pick' a 25-year span of gold returns. In 1980 gold closed at around $590 an ounce. In 2005, it closed at $513. During this decades-long span there were several significant periods of both boom and bust in the U.S. economy, so I think it is a good litmus test. (source: macrotrends.net and note these closing prices are not inflation-adjusted).

I try to invest in what I know. For example, I do not directly invest in any pharmaceutical or life sciences stocks because I know absolutely nothing about medicine, nor do I even have any interest. Plus, even if I had good information on a pharmaceutical stock, I would probably never invest in it directly anyway, as I feel a singular investment there would be too risky. I also barely ever invest directly in individual technology stocks. You may find this strange since my entire career has been in information technology, but I just find picking technology winners too complex and risky. I see it daily first-hand on my job how most technology is easily replicated and replaced by something newer and better, and likely cheaper. History has shown that most transformational technology has seen us replace very expensive solutions with very cheap solutions. Your cell phone is a great example of this. Another example is Zoom (ticker: ZM) stock. The stock has fallen horrifically from its all-time highs during Covid-19 lockdowns, and appears to have flatlined since pandemic lockdowns. Also, Zoom also has a lot of other competition in the video conferencing field. I get my technology exposure by investing in a technology mutual fund that I own called the Janus Henderson Global Technology and Innovation Fund (ticker: JATIX), which has returned about 20% per year over the last ten years. Later in the book, we will examine, in great detail, how non-technology stocks can often provide greater stock returns than technology stocks.

I know many investors that spend large chunks of their lives analyzing technology stocks to invest in, when, for example, you can just buy the Invesco QQQ Index Fund, which contains all the hottest tech stocks. Plus, in the QQQ you get exposure to Costco, Netflix and a few other great *non-tech* stocks. The QQQ, by the way, has averaged about a 20% annual return over the past ten years. It is important to note that tech stocks do not always outperform other 'vanilla' or 'boring' stocks. Case in point is Domino's Pizza (ticker: DPZ) versus Google/Alphabet (ticker: GOOG) since both their 2004 IPOs. Dominos has actually had a higher total return than Google, and mind you with less volatility, as Dominos currently has a stock beta less than Google's. Don't worry if you don't understand what beta is, as I spend an entire chapter discussing it in Chapter 19.

Another thing to consider as you formulate your investment 'game plan' is try to invest in what you are knowledgeable about, and the companies and industries that you believe in. They say you aren't supposed to get attached to a stock. Some say you are supposed to rent, and not own a stock for the long term. I do, however, get attached to quite a few stocks that I own. I confess, I may even be in love with many or most of the stocks and investments that I have. One thing I am proud of is that most all the individual stocks I own the company makes a profit. I prefer to invest in companies that are either at or near profitability. I like investing in the stock of companies that either pay a dividend and have established themselves. I look at it as I don't have to be the first investor in a company to make money on their stock. If you invested in Google, Apple, or Amazon stock even five years after they went public, and held them until today you still would have made a lot of money.

By investing in these early-stage tech startups later, I feel you remove a lot of the risk you might otherwise subject yourself to by being too early.

In developing your game plan in life, you might also want to consider how your brain thinks. Some highly successful people have told me to be in the 'attracting' business, not the 'chasing' business. You will expend less energy and anxiety, and just might be a lot happier. Having one hundred people love what you are doing, or making, is better than having one million people just 'like' it. Those one hundred people are your marketing department. And in the process, you might just attract money to yourself.

There is absolutely nothing wrong with flying coach on an airplane. But if you ever fly first class, you won't ever want to fly coach again. This is my personal experience and mindset I have in life. You should live with a sense of urgency and approach stock investing the same way. The stock market moves fast. One piece of stock investing 'advice' I would give is do not wait until you're seventy-years-old to learn about stock investing. It will likely be too late.

I'm good at blackjack, and I play when I'm in Atlantic City or Las Vegas. But if I walked into a casino and went in the poker room, I'd get destroyed. I know what I'm good at in life, and also what I'm not good at. In my opinion, most of the mental part of stock investing should take place **before** you even invest a penny in the stock market. Know what game you are playing. By the way, the stock market is a game. Do what you can do to get an edge. How to get an edge will be explored in the rest of this book. I like to approach the stock market in simple terms. I'm more of an 80% fundamental analysis investor, but I also look at technical and stock charts about 15% of the time. The remaining 5% I utilize mental, macro, and 'other stuff', with some of the 'other stuff' being common sense. I have found throughout life that, unfortunately, common sense isn't too common.

CHAPTER 2

FREE INVESTING INFORMATION – AND WHERE TO FIND IT

In the game of football, you're supposed to do all your work and thinking *before* the game starts. Pressing that *buy* button in your brokerage account to purchase a stock is like a football kickoff, and once kickoff starts, it's too late to be thinking. If someone, for example, plays professional football, and they are thinking during a game, watch what happens to them. A more extreme example would be the sport of basketball. There's barely any time to think during a basketball game, since the game moves so fast. Do all your thinking and information gathering before the game starts, be it a sport or, in the case of the stock market, buying a stock.

Free investment information is one of the foundations of this book, and the key is using it to your competitive advantage and attempt to earn a profit investing in the stock market. Imagine if Warren Buffett had access to the internet and Yahoo Finance in the 1950s.

The rest of the book will detail how to interpret the information in this chapter, and use it to make wise and safe investment decisions. There is so much stock information out there that you need to be careful to not let it overwhelm you. Keep in mind that entire books have been written on just about every chapter in ***Across The Street***. You have to work hard and dig deep to find the next Google or Amazon, as it's not just going to jump out at you. Personally, I spend maybe up to one hour every evening watching the free investment videos and the free investor information websites I will explain below. I also do this same routine 365 days a year, as I rarely take a day off. I'm not saying that you need to spend that much time every day doing investment research, it is just what works for me and what I enjoy doing. Somewhere buried in all these YouTube videos and investment websites mentioned below, I am convinced I can find the *next* Google or Amazon; speaking for myself, I just truly believe that. If you are investing on your own, you need to do the proper stock market research, which is the same thing any billion-dollar financial institution does when they purchase a stock.

There are two major schools of thought when it comes to approaching the markets and attempting to value stocks: fundamental and technical analysis (also known as "TA"). Both are important and both have their pluses and minuses. We will be discussing both in great detail in the coming chapters.

Fundamental analysis evaluates securities by attempting to measure their intrinsic value, whereas TA looks to statistical trends in the stock's price and volume. Some popular TA terms you may have heard are; moving averages, support and resistance levels, and trendlines. TA asserts that patterns often repeat themselves because investors often behave in the same way in the same situation. TA does not consider the underlying business, or the economics that affect the value of a company, whereas fundamental analysis does.

So where is all this headed in the future? Technology and artificial intelligence are rapidly moving this process forward. The fields of quantitative investing and behavioral finance have gained recognition in the asset management industry due to their more scientific approach, and this is likely where things headed.

I look at all the free investment information out there like a professional football coach preparing for a game. When an NFL coach prepares for a game, they have all the information of their opponent on video, and it is all free and available. You mostly know what the other team does because it is all there on video for the entire world to see each and every week during football season. Your football opponent basically hands you their playbook for free because all their games are on video. Just like the stock market, where you can get all the free information to help you. Finding the information is what this chapter is about. All you must do is watch it and process it. Every NFL football team also employs at least twenty or more fulltime coaches and management personnel, I am guessing. With all this collective knowledge, my NFL football team can't seem to barely win a game, and that always boggles my mind. I am probably making this sound too easy, but gathering all the stock information you can is a lot like preparing for an NFL football game. It is a scary reminder how difficult it is to win in the stock market and the NFL. Just having all the information, though, doesn't guarantee you will win in the stock market or the football field, but it is a great place to start. The rest of this book will help you interpret and use this information.

Information is key, but you can't always trust all the information that comes your way. In early 2021, finance company JPMorgan said Bitcoin could rally as high as $146,000 per coin in the long term, as it competes with gold as an alternative currency (as published in a CNBC article dated 1/5/2021). Then, just a couple weeks later, JPMorgan said that they thought Bitcoin would not reach $40,000 anytime soon (as published in Yahoo Finance on 1/25/2021). Be careful believing everything you hear and read.

Social media is influencing and dictating stock prices. The importance of this chapter is also supported by the following piece of information that was released in 2021, literally just as I was writing my first stock investing book, *Night Trading*. Global investment manager, VanEck Associates, had just introduced an exchange-traded fund that seeks to take advantage of commentary written about stocks on the internet. The VanEck Social Sentiment ETF (ticker: BUZZ) tracks an index of the 75 most-favorably mentioned companies on the web. The fund has an algorithm that goes through news outlets, social media and blogs. Even Wall Street has woken up to the critical importance that social media trends have on stock and crypto prices.

There is a wealth of free investment information online, both written and in videos. If you are a novice to stock investing, I would suggest to start out watching free online videos on any of the following legendary and successful investors (in no particular order): Warren Buffett, Peter Lynch, and John Bogle. Just Google any or all three investors and watch their many published videos online. I often listen to their videos in the morning when getting ready for work or eating breakfast. I also find myself lying in bed some nights and going to sleep listening to their videos on my cell phone. Whatever works for you; but just watch or listen to them.

> **Warren Buffett** is an American investor and the Chairman and CEO of Berkshire Hathaway. He is considered one of the most successful investors in the world.

> **Peter Lynch** is an American investor and former mutual fund manager. As the manager at Fidelity Investments between 1977 and 1990, Lynch averaged a 29.2% annual return, consistently more than double the S&P 500 stock market index.

> **John Bogle** was an American investor and founder and chief executive of The Vanguard Group. He is credited with creating the first index fund. Bogle preached investment over speculation, long-term patience over short-term action, and reducing broker fees as much as possible.

Below are some excellent and useful free investing tools that I recommend. While most of these sites have a free component that will work just fine for most, they almost all have a paid component as well, as dictated by your appetite for investment information. Nonetheless, get ready to get to know all the wonderful people on these valuable sites, because they're about to become your new best friends. Please note, they are in no particular order. Please search for the following YouTube channels:

> **The Compound** A channel for discussions about business, investing, economics, finance, and trading. They hold weekly shows interviewing top investors.

> **Kitco** The global precious metals authority. Recognized as the leading voice in commodities information providing best-in-class news, data, and insights. Their diverse team of journalists also report on the economy, stock markets, and cryptocurrencies.

> **CNBC television** CNBC is the recognized world leader in business news and provides real-time financial market coverage and business content consumed by hundreds of millions of people per month across all platforms. Their channel has short, mostly two-to-six-minute videos, which makes it easy

to consume. This is my favorite daily stock market channel.

Scott Melker: The Wolf Of All Streets One of the best Bitcoin and crypto channels. Really good chart and trend analysis. Excellent interviews with top crypto experts. The place where you can get the latest crypto news, market trends, and crypto trading advice.

Next are free websites I use for my investment research, and to find out the very latest investment and financial news. It is a mix of free and paid content but a lot of the good basic information you will need is free. You may need to turn off your adblocker on some of the sites. Please note, for the purposes of this book, that you do not need to subscribe to the paid version of these websites, as the free will work fine. If you feel the need for more information, then by all means subscribe to the paid versions. Note that these are in no particular order.

X (formerly Twitter) This might be the best place for free stock information. I use it a lot. Just use their Explore and Advanced Search features to find what you are looking for.

Investopedia The world's leading source of financial content on the web, ranging from market news to retirement strategies, investing education, stock research, and more.

Finviz This is one of my favorite investing websites. Their name stands for financial visualizations, and they provide financial research and analysis. They also have some of the nicest looking and useful stock charting software out there. I get practically all of my stock charts from here.

TheStreet Top-notch financial website. Great articles and videos. The company was co-founded by Jim Cramer.

Yahoo Finance One of the best financial websites, if not the best. Latest investor news as well as links to financial company articles on other websites. I use this site almost religiously, as it contains most of the financial information and metrics you need about a company. They also link to many Motley Fool articles, which contain some good investing information.

NY Post Business Good, interesting articles. I go to this site every day.

CNN Business Good business articles and accurate and useful financial information. All the latest stock news on every stock, including earnings, profitability, financial statements, and key financial ratios. Nicely shows a stock's one, three, and five-year returns.

247WallSt Can be used for stock analysis and some of their recommendations.

InvestorPlace I occasionally find stock tips here.

Tipranks TipRanks is a valuable tool for stock market investing. TipRanks is great because their experts do all the work. TipRanks is a comprehensive dataset of Wall Street analysts. They have become the go-to tool for part-time to professional investors. TipRanks is a source of objective facts amid all the opinion, spin, and conflicts of interest in the finance world. The Basic Plan is free on TipRanks. I use the Average Analyst Price Target to compare to the current price of a stock I already own, or if I am considering buying a brand-new stock. I also use some of the data in their Stock Analysis section. I find the data in here accurate and I compare it to the same data in Yahoo Finance, just to cross reference for accuracy. I caution you to keep in mind that stock analyst price targets for a stock are that analyst's opinion. So, ultimately, you must look at someone else's opinion as just that, an opinion.

Coinbase I go on here to check the latest crypto prices. The prices section also has top gainers and top losers and most trending cryptos. Coinbase also has a good learning section to teach yourself crypto.

Cointelegraph Cointelegraph is the leading independent digital media resource covering a wide range of news on blockchain technology, crypto assets, and emerging fintech trends.

CoinGecko CoinGecko provides a fundamental analysis of the crypto market. This is my 'go to' site for getting the latest crypto prices. You can also drill down and do analytics on many of the top crypto coins. They also have an excellent learning and educational section on crypto.

CoinDesk Crypto news, data, events, and education.

SOME FINAL THOUGHTS ON FREE INFORMATION, NETWORKING, AND STOCK INVESTING BOOKS

I received some free stock advice from someone I met and spoke with recently at an investor conference in Manhattan. This person is widely known and someone I have admired for several years. They speak often on the major financial networks about investing. He is one of the top hedge fund managers in the world, and someone I am always looking to soak up any stock investing advice from. He told me he made 90% of his wealth in only about 8 stocks over his entire thirty-five-year investing career. This resets your brain regarding stock investing. He also told me he's never met a billionaire that 'day traded' their way to a billion dollars. His opinion is it's best to find a few of the market leader stocks, and just sit on them for several years. The money is made in the sitting.

One thing I have learned is that a key to investing success is building your personal network with other like-minded investors and traders. This way, you can piggyback off their knowledge and expertise. You can let them do most, or all, of the stock research. For example, I have a close group of about five pro traders that I trust completely. They might send me a personal stock pick of theirs, and most of the time I will buy the stock just on their recommendation.

I would not be at the level of investing I am had it not been for my investing network, including friends, family, coworkers, other investors, people on Financial Twitter, etc. Always remember, nobody makes it in life only by themselves. Your network is the most important thing in investing, and life as well. You can lump our schools in there as well. Colleges and universities aren't only for education, they're for connection. When people pay for a Harvard MBA, they aren't just paying for the coursework, they're paying for the network. If used correctly, social media platforms like Twitter (now X), and even Reddit, offer access to just as valuable networks for free.

Now that we covered the free stuff, let us now discuss things that can help you immensely in stock investing that are *almost* free: stock investing books. Do you know why some people either do not invest, or over time end up losing money in the stock market? A large part of the reason is most people do not read stock investing books, and I have the evidence to prove it.

I enjoy reading all types of books, both fiction and nonfiction. According to publishing experts Self-Publishing School, the most popular and profitable book genres (or categories) on Amazon are romance, crime/mystery, religion, science fiction and fantasy. Throughout the years, romance continues to be the most popular and profitable book genre by far. Even if you look within nonfiction books, stock investing books fall well short in popularity to genres like: memoirs & autobiography, cooking, health & fitness, self-help, and motivational. If you do not believe this data, just head over to the book section of your local store, and tell me how many stock investing books you see. You might only see a few.

The return on investment, or ROI, of a $25 or $35 stock investing book could be enormous. You might belong to a gym, where you pay a monthly fee. I would argue the only thing in life other than a stock investing book that is a better use of your money is a gym membership. Your health might be the most important thing in your life. You may consider your $25 per month gym membership cheap. but keep in mind that is a monthly cost, while a book is only a one-time cost. A stock investing book has an advantage that it could make, or even save, you money.

I could take this conversation a step further. I think any good stock investing book should definitely be read more than once, just for the fact that the stock market and having success in stock investing are complex. I have a lot of stock investing experience, and education. Most of the stock investing books sitting here in my bookcase I have read multiple times, and I learn something new every time I read them.

If you paid $25 for a book and read it three times yourself, and then gave it to your partner to read, then to your friend to read. The book only cost $5, since it was read 5 times. Using this logic makes it clear that stock investing books are really 'dirt cheap' and underpriced. In my opinion, each additional reading of any book decreases its original cost. So, it is good to zoom out and have the mindset that in the grand scheme of things, stock investing books can be a great investment, because they can make, or hopefully worst case even save you money. The most expensive way to learn is trial and error. The cheapest way to learn is read books.

CHAPTER 3
BOOK VALUE PER SHARE

In simple terms, share prices are determined by supply and demand. The stock price is determined by the last price a buyer and seller agreed on. Hence, stock prices can change frequently, as buyers and sellers constantly negotiate new prices with each other. Each shareholder just owns a tiny piece of the entire pie, represented by a share. Imagine for a second that you owned a bookstore, and were looking to sell it. First, you'd have to figure out what it's worth. Maybe you'd add up the value of all the books in the store. Then factor in what the land and building of the store are worth. There could be other 'intangible' things that are valuable as well, like the name or brand recognition you've built up over the years. You might have a very recognizable logo for your bookstore that could be worth something too. So, you add all this up, subtract out all the liabilities that you owe and, voila, you have the total price that you can sell your bookstore for. All you need to do next is put up a for sale sign in front of your bookstore.

The price of a stock is just a representation of everyone's opinion at a point in time, and the price constantly changes. Many investors use book value per share to find undervalued stocks, and that is exactly what we will be discussing. We'll examine if there is any type of 'magic formula' that exists to help stock investors try to calculate the fair value of a stock, represented on a per share basis. That metric does exist, but is only useful in calculating the value of certain types of businesses, mostly brick-and-mortar type businesses. The metric some investors use to value a stock is called book value per share, abbreviated BVPS. We will learn all about BVPS, where it works, and where it is not applicable.

I've been using this BVPS metric for years to make a lot of money in bank stocks. Those bank investments will be analyzed in detail in the next chapter, but for now we have to learn the basics of BVPS. It does have limitations, but can be a great way to see what certain businesses might truly be worth if that business had to be liquidated and sold today. While BVPS may not be useful to the specific stock you are looking to buy, it is a great educational tool to learn a little bit about accounting and finance, and how to potentially value a stock.

Simply put, investors use BVPS to gauge whether a stock is valued properly. BVPS is a misused and misunderstood metric. BVPS represents the amount that you would theoretically receive as a shareholder should the company dissolve. It determines the potential value per share of a company in the event that it must liquidate its assets.

This metric has largely fallen out of favor, and the consensus is that BVPS is no longer a good measure. As the economy has shifted away from asset-intensive businesses and more towards knowledge-intensive companies, book value has become less relevant. One of the biggest drawbacks to book value is that it does not consider intangible assets, such as intellectual property, patents, goodwill, or company branding. Companies that rely heavily on human capital and intangible assets are much more difficult to value. Thus, a firm's balance sheet may not accurately reflect the value of these intangible assets, and what would occur if the firm sold all its assets.

BVPS is a strategy that focuses on finding the intrinsic value of stocks and, more specifically, on undervalued stocks because these have the potential to rise. As noted, it is rarely used because it is difficult to calculate accurately. However, all the major investment sites still calculate and report it, and post it all over their websites. But I can tell you it made me a lot of money in an investment I made in a bank stock that I discuss in great detail in the next chapter. First, however, we need to understand what BVPS is and how it's calculated. In certain cases, BVPS can be extremely useful. Just because something is perceived to be difficult doesn't mean it can't be useful. This chapter will show that sometimes in life you have to dig deep to find a diamond, but in the end it will be worth it. You must sift through a lot of useless information, but BVPS can still be useful in finding some hidden gems.

It can be very difficult in today's modern world to put a price tag on many service-oriented businesses. For example, companies like Facebook have no factories, warehouses, or inventories to speak of. Instead, they have servers, a bunch of computers for employees to use, and a few office buildings that they rent. That's it. To explain BVPS, it's best just to use an example of a company everyone knows and can relate to; Facebook. In the graphic below from MSN Money, Facebook is trading at $270 per share with a BVPS of $45 per share according to MSN Money. Personally, I like to use BVPS, and simply compare this to the current share price (so in this case $270 compared to $45). Be alert that many financial websites today not only have the 'raw' BVPS figure (in this case the $45), but they also might provide the price-to-book ratio. The price-to-book (P/B) ratio compares a company's market value to its book value. It's really just a different way of showing BVPS. You should know how they got these numbers, and how to manually calculate yourself. This is very easy and I will now show you how.

A company's P/B ratio is their current stock price per share divided by its book value per share. In this Facebook example, you just take $270 and divide it by $45. This gives a Price/Book value of 6 (see picture below). And if you multiply $45 times 6, you arrive at the $270 per share stock price. So, the math works.

FACEBOOK, INC.

NASDAQ: FB

US Markets Closed

270.50 ▲ +0.11 +0.04%

After Hours : 270.26 -0.24 -0.09%
February 12, 2021 4:46 PM EST. Delayed 15 minutes; NASDAQ. Currency In USD

| SUMMARY | FINANCIALS | **ANALYSIS** | OPTIONS | OWNERSHIP | COMPANY | HISTC |

KEY STATISTICS   GROWTH   PROFITABILITY   PRICE RATIOS

Revenue	85.96B	EBITDA	39.53B
Net Income	29.15B	Return on Capital %	19.92
Market Cap.	770.29B	Return on Equity %	25.42
Enterprise Value	708.86B	Return on Assets %	19.92
Net Profit Margin %	33.90	Book Value/Share	45.03
PEG (Price/Earnings Growth) Ratio	0.53	Shares Outstanding	2.85B
Beta	1.25	Last Split Factor (Date)	1:0 (-)
Forward P/E	23.87	Last Dividend (Ex-Date)	0.00 (-)
Price/Sales	0.00	Dividend Declaration Date	-
Price/Book Value	6.01		

So, what does BVPS and the P/B value tell us? And what is considered a good P/B ratio? Traditionally, any value under 3.0 is widely considered a good P/B value, indicating a potentially undervalued stock. But this is not gospel. Also, keep in mind that a company trading far under its book value could also have serious problems, and that could be why their stock is trading so low. These are all factors that must be considered.

Some find the P/B ratio to be a useful metric because it can provide a good way to compare a company's market capitalization to its book value. Market capitalization, commonly referred to as market cap, is the value of a company traded on the stock market. It is calculated by multiplying the total number of shares by the current share price. A company's market cap will fluctuate with its share price. A weakness in P/B ratio evaluation is that it fails to factor in things such as future earnings prospects or intangible assets.

This is exactly the case with our Facebook example. It seems ridiculous to think that the book value of Facebook is only $45 per share. Almost all the time, the BVPS you find on these websites is not useful for technology companies. For example, I just checked the BVPS of Google and it is $24, yet the stock is $167. And the BVPS of Apple stock is $4, yet Apple stock is trading at $228. This doesn't mean, however, that BVPS is *never* useful, because it is, and how to strategically use BVPS to your advantage will be discussed in detail in the next chapter. Let's finish the technical discussion below of BVPS, so we will have a solid foundation for the next chapter, where I use it to show how I made money, and potentially how you could use it to make money as well.

BVPS is best used as a comparison tool. It can be used to compare against the current market value of a stock, or against a company's competitors. You can just do a Google search to find this information. There is no particular website I can tell you to use to find this competitor information. I happened to get the data below here of Facebook's P/B ratio to its industry and competitors from a website called GuruFocus:

Facebook's P/B ratio is ranked lower than
63% of the 492 Companies
in the Interactive Media industry.
(Industry Median Price to Book ratio:
4.29 vs. Facebook: 6.12)

One might say from this analysis that Facebook stock is a bit overvalued (i.e.-the stock is trading a bit higher) in terms of comparing its approximately 6.0 P/B ratio to its industry median. Note: GuruFocus' calculation of P/B ratio of 6.12 is very close to the 6.0 we calculated. Unlike valuation ratios relative to a company's earning power such as the P/E ratio, the P/B ratio measures the valuation of the stock relative to the underlying assets of the company. The price-to-earnings (P/E) ratio measures a company's current share price relative to its per-share earnings. The P/E ratio will be discussed in much greater detail in Chapter 8.

We have proved that the P/B ratio does not work well, or even at all, for technology businesses or social media companies like Facebook. It is extremely difficult to accurately value many businesses in today's world, since we live in a world that consists mostly of *service* type businesses. BVPS works best for the businesses that earn most of their profit from their assets, like for example banks and insurance companies. BVPS is more accurate than looking at price-to-earnings ratio to value bank stocks, as bank earnings can easily swing back and forth from one quarter to the next due to unpredictable, complex banking operations. We will see that BVPS can still be extremely valuable in the next chapter.

JUST BUY YOUR BANK! - REFUSAL TO EARN ZERO PERCENT INTEREST

In the spring of 2020, I walked into my very fine bank here in New Jersey, Investors Bank. Investors Bank was a regional bank in the Northeast, with branches mostly in New Jersey and New York. I had a large amount of cash I wanted to put in a savings account. I wanted to make a decent return on my money, but also did not want to take on much risk. To my dismay, I got a hard lesson in how low savings rates were in the United States, since they were near zero at the time. Now I know what people were talking about when they said "cash is trash."

I went home from the bank, sat down, took a deep breath, and did some thinking. There must be a better way to earn a higher rate of return on my money, I thought. The bank was offering around .2% interest on a savings account, and zero percent on a checking account. For comparison, I remembered I had just purchased stock in a company for about $3,500. I checked and that stock had gone up ten cents recently in just one day of trading. I was able to make about $50 in just that one day due to the ten-cent rise in the stock price. I did some quick calculations to see what I would have earned if I put that $3,500 into a savings account at my bank. I calculated it would have taken me over two years to earn that same $50 on a $3,500 investment in a bank saving account!

The extremely low savings interest rate environment got me thinking - instead of investing my money in a Certificate of Deposit (CD) or savings account at my bank – why don't I just buy my bank? I don't mean literally buy the bank, but buy their stock, and have them pay me a dividend? At the time, Investors Bank was paying a little over 6% dividend, which was very high compared to their lousy near-zero savings account interest rate. And what is perceived as a safer and more risk-free place to put your money than a bank? Banks are very stable, kind of like McDonald's restaurants; and how often do you see a McDonald's go out of business or close? Never. And when was the last time you have seen a bank go out of business? If anything, they are always opening new banks. Here where I live in New Jersey it seems like there is a bank on every other block, and they are constantly building and opening new ones. The Great Recession of 2008 to 2009 was the last time banks failed in a major way. That was a long time ago, and it does not seem like the U.S government would let banks fail anymore.

At the time, the 6% plus rate of return that Investors Bank dividends were paying me, in comparison to the near-zero interest rate of savings accounts, was pretty darn good. Also, when I bought the bank stock it was beaten up from the Covid-19 stock market correction. The bank was paying me to keep my money with them, the dividend, while at the same time the stock was appreciating to trade at least at its book value, and eventually way beyond. At the time, The Federal Reserve was providing fiscal stimulus to the U.S. economy after the Covid-19 pandemic. And the they were lowering interest rates to accomplish this. My confidence that the stock would go up grew even further, so I bought even more shares of ISBC.

Book value per share was discussed in detail in the prior chapter. The concept of book value is important to stock investing. A company's book value is essentially its liquidation value if all its physical assets were sold, and all company liabilities covered. BVPS was a very important factor in my decision-making process to purchase ISBC stock, and I eventually doubled my money as the stock increased 100% in price. At the time I purchased ISBC stock its BVPS was $11, and the stock was trading around $7 when I first bought it. So, by this metric the stock was greatly undervalued.

Banks are sometimes a good sector to invest in because they are much easier to value than, say, a software company that has a lot of intangible assets. As discussed in the last chapter, the BVPS that you see on financial websites is almost always way too low, and not useful to analyze most companies. BVPS, however, can be very accurate in the banking and insurance industry. When you see a banking stock trading at well below the reported BVPS, the stock is a definite buy for me. I was 110% sure that ISBC was greatly undervalued, so, I bought it, and it has been one of my best and low-risk stock purchases ever.

This was also validated by the fact that there already existed several regional bank ETFs, or exchange traded funds, which are discussed in detail in Chapter 9. There are entire ETFs that track regional banks, so regional banks must be pretty important. I drilled down a bit and checked if ISBC was included in any of these regional bank ETFs. In my mind, that would validate them and give ISBC exposure if their stock was included in an ETF, or some market index. Luckily, ISBC was included in the holdings of the three major regional bank ETFs that I examined. ISBC also had a relatively low-risk beta of around 1.10. Stock beta is discussed in detail in Chapter 19.

At some point in this entire runup of ISBC stock, I became curious if the employees that worked at my local branch actually bought and owned the stock for themselves. One day I was inside one of their branches, and no other customers were there, and I asked their employees: Do you all own ISBC stock? Of course, they all answered yes! It appears that the people getting rich off Investors Bank, and many other banks, were the ones that **didn't** have their money deposited there, and instead owned the stock!

I still wasn't done making money on just Investors Bank. In fact, the fun was just beginning. I did further research and found other undervalued regional banks in other parts of the country that paid a solid dividend. Right around the time that I bought ISBC, I found a bank headquartered in Texas called Comerica Bank (ticker: CMA). Comerica and its measurables were almost an exact match to ISBC. I ended up buying Comerica stock at around the same time as ISBC. Comerica has also been a great investment for me, as the stock made me a 100% gain when I sold it.

There always exists the possibility that a regional bank could be targeted for buyout by a larger, nationwide bank. That could also boost the stock price. Not surprisingly, there had been speculation that Investors Bank and Comerica Bank could eventually be bought out. This is really nothing new for regional banks, or banks in general, as there is generally consolidation in the banking sector. A potential buyout of my banks would likely drive the price of the stocks up even more. Well, I didn't have to wait very long, because Citizens Financial Group (ticker: CFG) announced in July 2021 they were buying out Investors Bank. So, I only had to wait about one year for Investors stock to runup. Things got even better for me because it was a stock and cash buyout, so not only did my shares convert to Citizens Financial Group stock, I also received about $2,000 cash.

I would like to mention one other thing regarding bank stocks and interest rates; when I purchased ISBC stock, and at that time, interest rates were very low. Rates were projected to be on the rise, and this bodes well for bank stocks because bank stocks benefit from rising interest rates. Interest rates and bank profitability are connected, with banks benefiting from higher interest rates. When interest rates are higher, banks make more money by taking advantage of the greater spread between the interest they pay to their customers and the profits they earn by investing. Higher interest rates are generally a boon to the banks, since they borrow on a short-term basis and lend on a long-term basis. Also, interest rate increases tend to occur when economic growth is strong, which means a greater demand for loans. These are all good reasons why investment in these bank stocks will pay off even more, and provide good growth.

Let's sum up what we learned in this chapter. I bought two bank stocks that were very low risk, but which paid me very generous dividends to park my money and invest with them. They had a stock price that was well below their book value per share upon buying, and provided me with an over 100% return on my investment. The "bank that keeps on giving" story gets even better, though, because I still to this day own a good chunk of my Citizens Financial shares, which still pay a nice dividend. The stock eventually went down a bit but at time of writing has recovered nicely to near all-time highs. My regional bank investing goes in line with the investment advice of Peter Lynch to "invest in what you know." One of the fun parts of owning stock in my bank was driving past the bank branch every day to and from work. I remember driving past the bank and thinking how much bank (money) I was eventually going to make. Investing in my bank's stock has been one of my smartest and most lucrative investment ideas ever. It even kickstarted me to write this book. I like to call it "thinking out of the bank."

I sometimes appear on stock investing podcasts, and I have my own stock investing show on Twitter Spaces that I host around three times a year. This chapter was also in my first stock investing book *Night Trading*. While this chapter is titled *Just Buy Your Bank,* you can use the same logic to buy other stocks besides just a bank. I only used a bank to make my point, but myself and others that have read my books have extended it to other types of stocks. This chapter has attained a cult following of stock investors. People have had fun with it and substituted *Just Buy Your Bank* with: Just Buy Your Gas Station, Just Buy Your Grocery Store, Just Buy Your Pharmacy, Just Buy Your Insurance Company, etc. It has been fun hearing other investors use 'common sense' and try to analyze and possibly invest in stocks of companies that they actually use their products or services.

CHAPTER 5
FOCUS: THE KEY TO SUCCESS

focus

[fo • cus] noun

seeing the light at the end of the tunnel. ignoring the noise. putting energy into what is important. not where you are but where you want to be.

> *"All men's miseries derive from not being able to sit quiet in a room alone."*
>
> **BLAISE PASCAL**

This is the *mental* and *mindset* chapter of this book. I personally have the mindset that only a very small percentage of movies are good, only a very small percentage of restaurants are good, and only a very small percentage of stocks are good. If you go by the sheer number of movies, restaurants, and stocks that have existed over the course of history, you get a sense of what I mean. Not sure about you but I don't have time in life to watch bad movies, eat at bad restaurants, invest in bad stocks, etc. Our life is too short to waste time. I rarely go to the movie theater to see a movie. Why you ask? Because, in my opinion, most movies are not worth watching. Give me a good movie and I'll go watch it. Regarding restaurants, the National Restaurant Association estimates a 20% success rate for all restaurants. About 60% of restaurants fail in their first year of operation, and 80% fail within five years of opening. I am also a very 'picky' stock picker as well. Give me a good stock and I'll buy it. I am skeptical of owning most stocks, and I have a very narrow range of stocks that I would even consider investing in. To be honest, the failure rate of stocks is probably close to the failure rate of restaurants, if not worse. Extending on the food concept, I also have the opinion that most food at the supermarket might be unhealthy. Next time you visit your supermarket walk up and down the aisles and look at all the soda, snacks, cookies, processed food, etc. Do you think most of the food is unhealthy? I dig deeper into this topic that most stocks are bad long-term investments in Chapter 12, where I cite data and studies that prove the point. We will spend the rest of this chapter getting into the right mindset to try finding stock winners, and the rest of the book learning how to detect the small percentage of stocks that can be outperformers.

Without focus, you will hit your golf ball into the woods, burn your dinner, crash your car, etc. It is very easy to lose focus in today's world because there are so many distractions, the main distraction being your cell phone. There is a famous proverb I really like and it says: "The art of knowing is knowing what to ignore." I think this is appropriate not only in life, but also stock investing. In the next section, I will discuss and make an analogy that the mindset and process of driving a car is very similar to successful stock investing.

The focus required to be successful at stock investing is very similar to driving a car. Roads are not always a straight line, and some are winding. Stock prices do not always move up in a straight line either. While you are driving, you don't really want to look behind you too much. You also don't want to look down ever when you're driving. The point is you need to focus when you're driving, or you will likely crash your car.

There might be bad weather when you drive your car, and in the stock market that could be geopolitical or economic events. There are guardrails on the side of the road when you drive, and even some guardrails in stock investing like stop losses. A stop-loss order is a risk-management tool that automatically sells a stock once it reaches a certain price. There is even a good lesson to learn when you park your car in the garage. Buying and holding great monster growth stocks for years is like spending a lot of money on a car, but resisting the urge to take it out of the garage. You probably love driving your Lamborghini or Rolls Royce, but you're not going to be driving it to work every day. It's not practical. Most investors cannot handle the mental part of holding a potential 2, 5, or 10-bagger stock. You might be inclined to take that Lamborghini out for a spin. It would be tempting to drive your Lambo to work every day, but the car is not really made for that. Remember, you will not have a 10x return on a stock you own if you sell it any point *before* it's a 10x. In many cases, keep that great stock you own in the *garage*. By the way, my point about keeping your Lambo in the garage is warranted, because certain cities now have 'noise-detecting cameras,' with microphones, that dish out tickets for loud engines, like a Lamborghini. From what I've heard, these noise tickets are very expensive, sometimes much more than speeding tickets.

With cars, there are often certain years to avoid. For many makes and models of cars, there are recalls. Consumer Reports even puts out a report of the years to avoid owning certain model cars. I owned a popular SUV a few years back. I loved the car. It was the roomiest car I ever owned and it drove well. However, during the end of its life, even when it did not have that many miles on it, the car started having major engine problems. I researched and found out my model year was a 'bad year' for the car, as there were many major engine and drivetrain problems. There were a few other 'bad years' to own the car as well.

This concept of car recalls can be applied to certain stocks as well. A stock like Tesla (ticker: TSLA), for example, has had some great years and some bad years where it went down a lot. When driving, there are stop signs and traffic lights to deal with that require patience. If you think stock investing is easy, or tire of listening to all the people that say all you need is time and patience, know that Microsoft stock had a 15% TOTAL return from 2000-2015, and that was, and still is, a solid company. An investor might run out of both time and patience if they owned Microsoft stock during that fifteen-year time period. An investor should also be aware of the *opportunity cost* of what other stocks they could have invested in while Microsoft did nothing for 15 years. Opportunity cost is explored in great detail in Chapter 24.

THE LION

In the Spring of 2022, I boarded an Amtrak train in New York City to attend an awards dinner in Hershey, PA for Micah Parsons, star NFL defensive player for the Dallas Cowboys. Parsons is widely regarded as one of the most talented and recognizable players in the National Football League. His main job on the football field is to attack, hunt down and *sack* the opposing team's quarterback. I was invited to attend by a friend that lives in Hershey. I know this is a book about stock investing, but if you are reading this you should try to take this exact same Amtrak train out to Hershey, PA. A large part of the ride from Manhattan to Hershey is gorgeous and relaxing. Hershey is a beautiful town, and the home of Hershey Foods and Hersheypark, an amusement park. Sitting in a window seat once you crossover into Pennsylvania, the scenery becomes beautiful, as the train meanders through scenic farms and farmland in the countryside.

At the awards dinner, I sat only a few feet from Parsons, as he talked about *hunting* NFL quarterbacks, much like a lion hunts in the wild. When he said the word *hunting*, my ears immediately perked up. He discussed how most of the time you never sack the quarterback the first, second, or even third attempt. He said it often is much later in the game when every-one begins to tire that his chances of sacking the quarterback increase. If you get time, go watch a nature video of a lion trying to catch a gazelle. Swift, agile, and capable of impressive leaps, the gazelle presents a formidable challenge for its predators. Lions rarely catch them because the gazelles run 50-60 miles per hour. Lions are fast, but are a shade slower than the leaner gazelles. Quite frankly, if you were a gazelle and another animal was chasing you to eat you for dinner, I'd imagine you would be running extra fast too. The lions, though, have a better chance catching wounded or tired gazelles. Maybe you can find a *wounded* stock? We will be discussing in upcoming chapters how to find *wounded* stocks. By the way, Parsons has actually nicknamed himself "The Lion," being that he played college football at Penn State University, where their mascot is the eastern mountain lion and named the Nittany Lion)

OVERTHINKING and UNDERTHINKING

If you can do these 3 broad, overall things, I think you give yourself a chance to be successful in the stock market. None of them, in my opinion, are that difficult either.

1. Read stock charts. (this is discussed in depth in Chapter 22).

2. Have common sense.

3. Be very selective and only focus on a few of the best quality companies and stocks.

In my opinion, the two biggest problems people have in stock investing are overthinking, followed closely by underthinking. We all know what overthinking means, but evidently, 'underthink' is technically not even considered a word in Webster's online dictionary. Some might loosely define underthinking as; giving insufficient thought or consideration to, or failing to consider adequately. Underthinkers are people who tend not to give important decisions, situations or even their own emotions enough mental attention.

Below are two real-life, detailed examples of overthinking and underthinking, as they relate to stock investing. These are two stocks that went up considerably over the last several years. There are quotes below about each stock, hypothetically describing someone's mindset and thinking, followed with a brief explanation as to why they never bought each stock.

AN EXAMPE OF UNDERTHINKING

Nvidia (ticker: NVDA) - "Nvidia stock is way overpriced. I'm not buying it."

Nvidia is currently one of the top semiconductor chip companies. I have never owned nor do I currently own Nvidia stock. On the night of May 24, 2023 Nvidia Corporation reported earnings after the closing bell. The stock had been doing well that year and from a p/e ratio perspective, was still considered 'pricey' (p/e ratios are discussed in more detail in Chapter 8). Nvidia reported better than expected earnings, but what happened right after that no one could have predicted happening. Nvidia blew investors away with its guidance, calling for $11 billion in revenue for the second quarter, compared to the analyst consensus of $7.2 billion. The stock jumped in afterhours trading, and the following day was up 25% on the excellent earnings report and future revenue guidance. The point here is that no matter how good you think you are at reading stock charts, no chart can predict the future. I did not own Nvidia stock, and that was my fault. The problem is me, the investor: I 'underthinked.' I thought the stock was overpriced. I didn't do enough research on Nvidia and the semiconductor industry to fully understand how dominant Nvidia was, and I didn't buy Nvidia stock. Nvidia stock closed that day up about $75.

AN EXAMPLE OF OVERTHINKING

> **Celsius Energy Drink (ticker: CELH)** - "Celsius has way too many competitors to ever be a dominant player in the energy drink space. Their stock will never go up a lot."

Celsius is an energy drink company, and at one point one of the best performing stocks of all-time, following in the footsteps of Monster Energy drink. Full disclosure: I was an 'early-ish' investor in Celsius stock. It is interesting to note that as Celsius stock was having its big runup that Tesla stock, an extremely popular and well-known company, was going down a lot. I thought Celsius stock could be an even better risk/reward investment than investing in Tesla, mostly because you don't have to take out a loan to buy a can of Celsius. With Celsius stock, in my opinion, you don't have to worry about all the other nonsense that other investors worry about, like high interest rates and high inflation. Celsius is what many consider 'affordable luxury,' as the average purchase price for one can is only around $2, and even cheaper on Amazon. The number of institutional holders of the stock has also been compounding. In my opinion, there is still a big runway for Celsius to grow their market share, and for the stock to possibly continue rising. Not surprisingly, as Celsius is growing, their main competitor Monster Energy drink's stock has been dropping. With my Celsius investment, I became more of an expert in the energy drink market than the Celsius stock chart. Many stock 'experts' say you have to invest in 'wide moat' businesses. Celsius had NO damn moat. Celsius had like 1% market share, and, even now, as they are more of a mature company, they have only around 10% of the energy drink space market share. Celsius has been one of the highest returning stocks of all-time, at time of this writing, up a little over 2,780% the past five years.

Warren Buffett said "it's crucial to understand that stocks often trade at truly foolish prices, both high and low. Efficient markets exist only in textbooks." I remember in the summer of 2022 going for the first time to eat at fast-food chicken restaurant Wingstop (ticker: WING) with my teenage son and a few of his friends. I didn't think the food was that good or anything special. I recall going back to my computer that night and doing some stock research on Wingstop. I wanted to look at their financials and their valuation. The stock traded at around $75 back then. After doing some of my usual stock research, I concluded the stock was overvalued. I even tweeted the next day that I wouldn't recommend buying the stock. Fast forward two years later to the time I am writing this, and Wingstop stock is trading at around $420 per share. My original thesis on Wingstop stock was completely wrong, as the stock did over a 5x in just two years. The lesson here is that it's better to learn early in your stock investing career that the stock market doesn't make any sense. If it made sense, everyone would be multi-millionaire stock investors. People want the stock market to make sense because it's human nature that we want things in life to make sense. It is also human nature that we want to prove ourselves right in life. You could be the smartest stock investor in the world, but the stock market is a grouping of millions of other smart stock investors too, and they all have their own biases. Stock prices are just people's opinions at a point in time. The stock market typically does the opposite of what you think it will do. As Charlie Munger told Warren Buffett during the 2015 Berkshire Hathaway annual shareholder meeting: "If people weren't so often wrong, we wouldn't be so rich."

TENNIS AND STOCK INVESTING

There are parallels between tennis and stock investing. Stock investing has many similarities to tennis, a sport I played in my childhood and in high school. I played tennis from around age seven until age eighteen. As a young child, I dreamed of playing professional tennis one day. Tennis is a very mentally taxing sport. Tennis is you versus you. Tennis can be a very lonely sport, as can stock investing. I spent a large part of my childhood hitting a tennis ball by myself against a concrete wall near our house. In tennis, players try to overcome anxiety by blocking out images of possible failure and concentrating solely on the ball, swinging as normally as they can. This is the reason this is in the focus chapter of this book. I was the captain of my high school tennis team. Prior to high school I had played five sports year-round: baseball, basketball, soccer, swimming, and tennis. By the time I entered high school I quit all those other sports to focus solely on tennis. Spoiler alert: I never became a professional tennis player as I stopped playing in college, but the sport taught me a lot, and I don't regret those long, hot summer days of my youth playing tennis. I also had no idea at the time that tennis would eventually help me become a better stock investor.

Winning over 100 events and 20 major men's singles titles, including a record eight Wimbledon championships, Roger Federer is one of the best tennis players in the sport's history. Roger Federer played 1,526 singles matches throughout his career, and won nearly 80% of them. However, he only won 54% of the individual points within those matches. To put it another way, one of the greatest tennis players of all time barely won over half the points he played throughout his storied career. Think of an up day in the stock market as a tennis point won and a down day as a point lost. An examination of data from 1950 to 2023 revealed that the market was up 54% of all trading days —the same *exact* percentage as Federer's points won.

In investing, it is important to stay aware of the current environment of the stock market, be it a bull or bear market, and be ready to make small adjustments as things change. You can diversify your stock portfolio with dividend stocks, technology stocks, or even gold or Bitcoin. In tennis, you can make things more challenging for your opponent if you use a variety of shots during a match: drop shots, lobs, slices, and ball placement.

Tennis can serve as a blueprint for how one can approach stock investing, and life. Tennis is very demanding and brings structure, as does stock investing and stock trading. Both require you to focus and tune out all distractions. Imagine back in the day playing John McEnroe in tennis, a player famous for his temper tantrums. I'm sure that McEnroe meant to distract his opponents. Likewise, investors must tune out distractions, both internal and external. Headline news, or watching CNBC, for example, can make you question your investment decisions. The key is knowing what is relevant to your goals, and tuning out the rest.

The best tennis players have a variety of shots in their toolbox. You need your dominant shots, and the wherewithal to mix up your approach when necessary. In investing, this is called diversification. Diversification is discussed in detail in Chapter 11. You'll often hear diversification described as "not putting all of your eggs in one basket." When one of your stocks eventually has a 50% or more drawdown, you will be glad you owned other stocks in your portfolio. Speaking of lob shots in tennis, the lob was my favorite shot. I used to love it when my opponent would come to the net. I got great satisfaction watching them run backwards at a high rate of speed, knowing full well they would never catch up to the ball I had just lobbed over their head.

Both a tennis player and a stock trader's process are extremely important, because often that is all you can lean on. Tennis players regularly lose a string of points, and stock traders and investors can see their favorite stock they own have a large drawdown. This simply means there are always certain things that are out of your control, but what we can control is our process. Remember, as we just learned, one of the greatest professional tennis players of all-time only won 54% of the individual points within all his matches, and still was an overall winner.

To conclude this chapter on money and mindset, we can look to a recent interview that champion trader, and stock investing book author, Mark Minervini gave to Investor's Business Daily. Unlike sports, he says, where physical attributes, such as being bigger and stronger or jumping higher or running faster than someone else can provide an edge, there's no genetic advantages in stock trading. "I don't believe there's a natural born trader," Minervini said. "I think traders are developed."

CHAPTER 6

WHERE ARE THE CUSTOMERS' YACHTS?

F red Schwed Jr. was an American stock broker turned author, known for his book on Wall Street, *Where Are the Customers' Yachts? or A Good Hard Look at Wall Street.* The title of this 1940 book refers to a story about a visitor to New York who admired the yachts of the bankers and brokers. Naively, he asked where all the customers' yachts were. Of course, none of the customers of the bankers and brokers could afford yachts, even though they followed the advice of their bankers and brokers.

Many consider a financial advisor just a salesperson for financial companies. I personally know a financial advisor at one of the largest brokerage firms in the world. They have done very well for themselves, owning a million-dollar second house at the New Jersey shore, along with a nice boat. I'm not knocking this person, but whenever we speak, I joke why do people even need you if they could simply put all of their savings in a S&P 500 Index fund and likely beat the returns that they or any investment professional could achieve? And at a much lower cost. This is the same person who never heard of Bitcoin nor advised any of their clients to allocate some of their funds, even a microscopic amount, to Bitcoin several years ago, or even now. Bitcoin, by the way, has been one of the best-performing assets over the last ten years. This financial advisor is a great person, but I've never sought financial advice from them as I act as my own financial advisor. I'm not saying you have to dump your financial advisor, if you have one, but I wrote this book to give you the information to make informed investment decisions yourself at the lowest possible cost. Hopefully, a cost that is zero or close to zero. If you don't believe me, then listen to Warren Buffett. Buffett states in his past annual reports, and even spoke at the 2017 Berkshire Hathaway Annual Meeting, that most financial advisors don't deserve their fees. Buffett says that, for most professions, you do get value added by hiring a professional. He gives an example and an analogy that you would pay an obstetrician to deliver your baby, as opposed to just having a stranger off the street deliver it. Same thing with hiring a plumber or a dentist, for example, as you would want someone that you can be absolutely certain they will solve your problem. But would you, for example, give a lot of money to your mechanic before they even worked to fix your car problem if they told you they weren't really sure if they could fix it? For reasons unknown, some people do this with stock advice.

Buffett's argument when it comes to hiring a personal financial advisor, though, is that the odds are highly stacked against them in aggregate being able to outperform the S&P 500 Index. The financial advisor's annual compensation fee subtracted from their return, he says, usually will not beat the S&P 500 annual return that you could get on your own. Buffett himself even advises people to just invest in an S&P 500 Index fund. I do think, though, most people should hire a highly skilled tax advisor or CPA to help manage your taxes. "You have to have tax efficiency because you don't get the dollars you earn, you get the dollars you keep," explains famous life coach and author Tony Robbins.

If you are currently not up to speed on stock investing, then this book, at the very least, should help to educate you so you can have an intelligent conversation with a certified financial advisor. Or, if you simply do not have the time or trust yourself to manage your finances, then by all means hire a certified financial advisor – it might help you sleep better at night. By the way, my friend who manages money at the brokerage firm, when I asked him where his firm invests their clients' money, he told me "mostly in index funds." You must wonder if you can just invest in index funds yourself. We will discuss index funds in detail in Chapter 9.

CHAPTER 7

BUY WHAT YOU KNOW... AND WHAT'S HOT

Peter Lynch, the former head of the Fidelity Magellan Fund, is one of the most well-known investors of all-time. He has a unique investment approach where he invests in "understandable" stocks. Lynch's approach is strictly bottom-up, selecting from companies with which the investor is familiar, then through fundamental analysis that emphasizes a thorough understanding of the company. Lynch says the more familiar you are with a company, and the better you understand its business and competitive environment, the better your chances of finding a winner. Lynch advocates looking for and investing in companies with which one is familiar, or whose products or services are relatively easy to understand. With Lynch's way of investing there is no formula or screen that will produce a list of prospective stocks.

Lynch's bottom-up approach means that prospective stocks must be picked one-by-one, then thoroughly investigated. Lynch suggests that investors keep alert for possibilities based on their own experiences, such as within their own business or job, or simply as a consumer of products. To clarify, Lynch never meant that every company you know about is a great stock to invest in. The stock must be investigated, and in the next chapter we go over fundamental stock analysis in detail to help you accomplish this.

When I say to invest in what you know, I need to clarify it is also *who* you know, not always necessarily what you know. This could actually be the most important and useful chapter in **Across The Street**. I say this because looking back at my life of buying a lot of stocks, most of my best investments and advice came from either using a company's product or getting stock tips from friends. The advantage you give yourself is that you already know and have information on the product.

To clarify and summarize what I mean; buy who you know, buy what's hot, buy what you use, or buy what you know. We will now dig into all four:

Buy Who You Know

Now that you are armed with all the free investment information from Chapter 2, you are ready to start building out your network of stock tips. Finding the *right* stocks to buy is a lot like looking for a job – it is mostly who you know. You need to "plug yourself in" to a stock tip network. Start from within your inner circle and build out. The stocks that I have had the greatest returns on in my life have come from advice and tips from friends, family, or work acquaintances. They either read or heard about a stock on the news, from browsing the web, or even from a friend or co-worker themselves. The best thing about this kind of investment information is that it is totally free.

Start with your friends and family first. Then build out to friends of friends and friends of their friends; and so on. Next, move on to conversing with your co-workers at your office. Then, vendors or customers that you deal with at your day job. There is so much stock information out there in the world, and everyone is so connected via social media that you will be surprised how much there is to sort through and process.

I recommend that you interact with people of all ages as well. Get out of your comfort zone. I got interested in Bitcoin from an employee at my company that just graduated college, so he was much younger than me. Conversely, if you are currently very young and just starting out investing, you should seek out advice from much older people as this will give you an entirely different perspective. That Bitcoin tip from my much younger coworker made me a 400% return in less than one year. Just keep building out your 'stock tip tree' branch by branch.

The best example I can cite of a great stock tip was one I received from a software vendor in 2020. I casually told him that after the global pandemic I was looking to invest in an airline stock after they had all tanked, but I didn't know which one to buy. I had just started researching the top six or seven airlines and was also looking at the financial condition of each. He told me not to worry about it, as he had just done his own extensive research on all the major airlines and told me to just buy Delta Air Lines. I did that day, and the stock ended up doubling.

Buy What's Hot

Another piece of advice is maybe to go with what's hot. This sounds simple, and it is. To be a little more specific, what's hot could also mean investing into sectors or trends where there is momentum. Although it is more difficult, you also want to try to predict what is *going to* be hot. This could give you more stock gains if you can get in on a stock before everyone else does. One way to do this is interact with younger people. The younger kids and generation are more tuned in to the latest fads and trends. I have two teenagers so I sometimes take a peek at what things they are into. If you only invest in what you know, then you could potentially miss out on something you don't know, and what's hot as well. Maybe what is hot could be the shoes your kids are wearing. In short, you don't want to fight the trend, as it could be your friend.

Finally, the thesis regarding about maybe investing in what is hot can be supported by a quote from famous investor Charlie Munger. Munger said: "The first rule of fishing is fish where the fish are."

Buy What You Use

It amazes me how sometimes the most lucrative and simple investments are staring us right in the face, or in this case right under your feet. Back in 2021, I spent a couple weekends walking on the boardwalk at the New Jersey shore, and every plank of every boardwalk as well as almost every house I passed used synthetic decking, trim, and railing. At the time, lumber prices were through the roof and housing demand was high, so it's understandable people were using mostly synthetic decking and planking that basically lasts forever.

Around that time, I decided to buy some stock in a company called Azek (ticker: AZEK) and it appreciated nicely for me. The AZEK Company is a designer and manufacturer of beautiful, low maintenance and environmentally sustainable products focused on the fast-growing outdoor living market. Azek is one of the market leaders in its industry, as its main competition is another great company that you probably heard of called Trex (ticker: TREX). Trex and Azek are the two publicly traded market leaders in the wood-alternative composite decking and railing space. They both sell an easy-to-understand product that is very much needed and in demand. I was also familiar with their product as I used it on my wraparound porch at my house over ten years ago and it still looks brand new to this day. There is no need to ever paint it, and I only power wash it once a year to clean. At the time, Trex stock was trading at double Azek's share price. Trex was also trading at a fairly high valuation, a little too rich for me, so I was hoping my Azek stock just simply followed the same trajectory as Trex and Azek could one day double in price. Remember the title of this chapter: Buy what you know. It's just common sense sometimes. Unfortunately, Azek (ticker: AZEK) stock ended up being a loser for me. Azek stock price ended up falling into the teens in 2022, when the entire stock market had a major downward correction. The good news if you bought at those lows, the stock went on to triple in price at the time I am writing this.

Another example of 'buy what you use' is my Uber stock investment. I started buying Uber (ticker: UBER) stock in 2022. I had been using them for ridesharing. They only really have one notable competitor, and their app (along with your credit card) is on most everyone's cell phone in the world. To say the least, unless something drastic or completely destructive happens to their business model, Uber stock is one of those stocks in my portfolio that I want to keep holding. They also have a lot of room to grow more internationally, as well.

Buy What You Know

I just discussed my investment in Celsius energy drink stock in detail in Chapter 5. It is the perfect "buy what you know" stock, so I'm going to discuss my personal investment in them in a bit more detail now, in hopes that you can learn how to find these winning stocks yourself.

I am friends with a highly successful growth stock investor. One of those people that always seems to be an early investor in the current, or next, hot thing. They spend a lot of time at the gym, and found a couple huge stock winners from products he saw people using or wearing there. This person was a very early investor in an energy drink everyone drank, and also a pair of popular sneakers everyone at the gym wore. These two products were Celsius energy drink (ticker: CELH) and On sneakers (ticker: ONON). I personally met this person at an investor's conference in 2021, where I tried the energy drink and was instantly hooked on their flavors. Upon returning home from the conference, I started buying Celsius stock. I even did my own 'boots on the ground' sales research on the drink. On a scorching hot summer Saturday, I headed over to my local 7-Eleven convenience store to investigate who was buying Celsius energy drink. It was only 11:30am in the morning but about ninety degrees with ninety percent humidity. So, I parked myself near the cooler section in the back to 'spy' on buyers. I observed a bunch of people coming in and purchasing Celsius. Many of them were just buying Celsius and nothing else, not any food or anything. I interpreted this as positive for the stock, if they came in just to buy this particular energy drink.

One common thread of companies like Celsius or On is they both have what would be described as a 'cult following.' You could say the same thing about Tesla, or e.l.f. Beauty (short for EyesLipsFace). All these stocks have a large following on social media platforms, and their stocks have seen very large price appreciation. By the way, On eventually became hugely popular, and their stock ended up skyrocketing up about 50% for the year.

What if Alex Rodriguez (A-Rod) Listened to "Buy What You Know"?

Alex Rodriguez, better known as 'A-Rod,' made $455 million in career baseball earnings during his 22-year major league baseball career which began in Seattle, according to sports contract database Spotrac. Rodgriguez, though, recently said he regrets not buying some of those Seattle-based 'local' stocks at a young age. The three stocks he is talking about that were, or still are, headquartered in Seattle, where he spent many years playing baseball are: Microsoft (ticker: MSFT), Starbucks (ticker: SBUX), and Amazon (ticker: AMZN). He also made at least an additional $35 million in endorsements over that time. Let us analyze the numbers to see if Rodriguez is right about investing in the local stocks. Keep in mind, we are just speculating that he bought these stocks. You are about to be amazed at what we find, though.

Rodriguez made his major league baseball debut on July 8, 1994 in Seattle. Let us work the numbers from when he was a little bit older and had more money to invest, say in 1997. I used the free website *ytdreturn* to calculate his potential stock returns. I chose the date May 15th, 1997 as the 'from' date, just because it is the day Amazon went public. Also, he had just signed a $10.7 million contract extension then, so I hypothesized he invested $250,000 into each of three local stocks that were headquartered where Rodriguez's baseball team the Seattle Mariners played. I feel that $750,000 is a justifiable amount at the time for him to invest, since it was less than 10% of his entire $10.7 million contract. So, in my opinion, it would not be unreasonable for him to invest that much, even at that time. I ran the numbers to May 15, 2024, so a total of 27 years.

Microsoft would have returned around $11 million, Starbucks $13 million, and Amazon a staggering $521 million.

Note that this includes all dividends reinvested for Microsoft and Starbucks. Stock splits are also accounted for as well. So, the approximate grand total of $545 million in stock gains is roughly $55 million *more* than Rodriguez's *entire* career baseball salary and endorsement earnings of approximately $490 million. It is mind-blowing to think that if Alex Rodriguez invested just a microscopic amount of his baseball salary in those three stocks in 1997, he would have made far more money than his lifelong baseball salary and endorsements. This shows you the power of compounding and being in the 'right' stocks.

You may not have even been born when Rodriguez did my *hypothetical* investment into the 'Seattle stocks,' so fast forward decades later. Let's assume you waited until 2014 to invest in those three local stocks. Here are the results.

Approximate total stock returns for the 10-year period from July 2014 thru July 2024:

Amazon = +1,100%

Microsoft = +1,200%

Starbucks = +127%

As you can see, Starbucks stock is the laggard here. But, I'm pretty sure you still would have taken the large returns all three of these stocks provided in just ten years. What is even more interesting about all these stocks is they have a beta, or volatility, of right around 1.0, which is the same beta as the

S&P 500 Index. The concept of beta is discussed in detail in Chapter 19.

In summary, what we have learned in this chapter is that the best stock investments could be under your feet (Azek), under your butt (Uber), or right under your nose (Celsius). One of the main benefits of "buy what you know" is you don't have to do much stock research, because you already know the company. My Celsius stock investment that was discussed in detail in this chapter proved the four principles of: buy who you know, buy what's hot, buy what you use, and buy what you know, in just *one* stock. You don't always need to get a hit on **all four** of these, but as was just proved, it could be very powerful if you do.

CHAPTER 8
7 MINUTE ABS: ANALYZING A STOCK IN 7 MINUTES

"You can develop your own stock detection system outside the normal channels of Wall Street."

PETER LYNCH

One of the greatest business ideas might have been the "7 Minute Abs" idea from the movie *There's Something About Mary.* You should look up the 2-minute clip of that part of the movie on YouTube, as it is quite funny. 8-Minute Abs was an exercise video program from the 1990s that promised great abs if you followed their exercises for only 8 minutes a day. In all seriousness, though, I have developed my own 'stock detection system' for analyzing any stock in just 7 minutes. I use it religiously, and I've gotten so good at it I can now perform stock analysis on any stock in even less than 7 minutes most of the time.

Many people talk about stock investing success as being "mostly mental," but if that were true then Dr. Phil and Dr. Ruth would be the best stock investors ever. I think investing is 'some' mental, but I believe stock investing is "mostly being

ACROSS THE STREET FROM WALL STREET

in the right stocks." And if you want to be in the right stocks, you first need to analyze a stock.

I'm not into penny stocks, those defined as under $5 per share. I look for highly liquid stocks too. I'm not interested in low float stocks that trade under 500,000 shares per day either. The reason is this: If you're holding one of these low float stocks and everyone (large institutions, hedge funds or other large stock holders) decides to dump all their shares one day, who will be there to buy all those shares? Because if no one buys them after they're sold, it will be near impossible for the stock to go up again.

I am more of a fundamental (FA) stock investor. I'd say 80% of my investing thesis is FA. I also like that the word fundamental contains the word 'mental' because that too is a part of stock investing. You need offense and defense to win a football game and need fundamental and technical stock analysis to win the stock investing game. I believe the technicals follow the fundamentals in stock investing, and in Chapter 22 I do a deep dive into technical analysis. Whether you use fundamentals, technicals, or a combination of both, keep in mind what legendary investor William O'Neil said; "The only good stock is a stock that goes up."

One key concept you should take away from this chapter is that valuation matters. If you were to look at the stocks I currently hold in my portfolio, you would find that none of them would be considered overvalued. None trade at what you would describe as a 'crazy' valuation. Sure, a stock could keep going up even if the stock is already trading at what most would consider a very high price. But if the stock were to come back down, and if you bought early and your average cost per share is relatively low, you won't have to panic when the stock drops. This is called having a 'cushion.' I currently own some stocks that are perceived to have a high valuation, but I didn't buy them when they had a high valuation. Hence, I am not very worried if the share price goes down.

One way to learn almost everything you need to know about a company is to read their annual and quarterly reports. Publicly traded companies in the U.S. are required to file a host of documents with the Securities and Exchange Commission (SEC). They must complete both an annual report and 10-K yearly. The annual report is a user-friendly publication, while the 10-K is intended for investors and analysts. What I often read first, though, and give more weight to is the Investor Deck. I find it much more interesting and impactful. To find this document you just go to the company's website and head over to the Investor Relations section. From there you usually click on 'Events and Presentations' and it will usually be called Investor Deck. You will find what is around a 25-page PowerPoint presentation that you can download into a .pdf format. Here you will learn many interesting things about the company, including the Board of Directors. These are the people that, at a very high level, manage the company. You can see the job titles and company names that the Board members work at or have been employed. Sometimes, you will find that many were employed at large, popular, Fortune 500 companies and can bring a great skillset to the table. You will also find many more valuable things in the Investor Deck, including; the company's competitive advantages, detailed growth plans, growth strategy, and strategic plans.

Here is a list of 10 things I look for in my stock research. And they are not hard to observe and I find them all for FREE, mostly in all the places I discussed in Chapter 2: Free Investing Information. Note that the following are in no particular order.

1. **52 Week High/Low – look at where stock trading relative to its 50 and 200-day MA**

    Good to 'take a peek' and see at what price the stock has traded at in the past year and where it is trading at today. Digging a bit deeper, it is helpful to look at where the stock is currently trading in relation to its 50-day and 200-day moving averages. This can easily be found on the Yahoo Finance website for free, as well as on the website Finviz. Moving averages are discussed in detail in Chapter 22.

2. **P/E Ratio and Forward P/E**

    The price-to-earnings (P/E) ratio measures a company's current share price relative to its per-share earnings. Peter Lynch says the P/E ratio is a good indicator of how the market views a stock. Or, how much investors are willing to 'pay up' for the stock. Warren Buffett claims one of the most important things he ever learned from Charlie Munger was to buy quality stocks, even if you must pay up. A company with a low P/E could be undervalued, but it could also mean the market thinks that company will have little to no earnings growth in the future. A company with a high P/E could be overvalued, but it could also mean the market puts a premium on that company's earnings because they expect earnings to be higher in the years to come. A quality stock that trades at a P/E higher than what you think is 'normal' could mean the market has high confidence the company will increase its earnings. Do you think earnings of a company are important? I do, but that's just my opinion. I look at the P/E ratio because it contains a very important thing: earnings. After all, isn't a company in business to make money? Over time, a stock is going to be highly correlated to its underlying earnings. Be mindful, though, when looking at a company's current P/E ratio that, in fact, the market could be right. Lynch says that in the long run stock prices tend to follow earnings. Given Peter Lynch's track record in the stock market, I'd tend to agree with him. There is a lot of debate about P/E ratios. Some investors don't even pay attention to them. I, personally, use them to get a general read on the 'price-iness' of a stock. From my experience, I would say most people pay more attention to the forward P/E. The forward P/E ratio (or forward price-to-earnings ratio) divides the current share price of a company by the estimated future ('forward') earnings per share (EPS). For valuation purposes, a forward P/E ratio is typically considered more relevant than a historical P/E ratio. I use both, but I lean more toward looking at the forward P/E.

3. <u>Stage Analysis by Stan Weinstein</u>

Stan Weinstein outlined the principles of stage analysis in his 1988 book, *Stan Weinstein's Secrets for Profiting in Bull and Bear Markets.* In the book, he talks about the 4 stages of a stock, and when the optimal times are to buy or sell. It is actually a very simple concept to pick up and understand. Visually, you can see it here:

The goal is to buy a stock as it kicks off an established uptrend in stage 2. It's easy to visualize, but far more difficult to process it in real-time. If you don't have time to read the book you can just go to this extremely useful website I found, nextbigtrade, which explains the principles of stage analysis. The creator has also developed an amazing free stage analysis 'screener,' where you simply just enter a stock ticker symbol, and it gives you a wonderful graphic as to what stage the stock is currently in. There is even a visual on this website that shows stage analysis in action and explains the basics of it, including many examples.

4. **Is The Company Profitable?**

I personally only like investing in stocks of companies that are at or near profitability. I like to look back at the last five years of earnings. Predicting future earnings is difficult at best, so you have to go by what has already happened. Many of the free websites I discussed in Chapter 2 can provide this information. You must be cautious when looking at profitability, however, because companies can pull many levers to affect their reported earnings per share. That said, I put more weight in the company's revenue, because you can't really 'manufacture' or manipulate your revenue. I'm not saying to only buy stock in companies that are profitable, but it helps me narrow down my investment choices and it works for me. Remember, Amazon was not profitable when it went public back in 1997, and it took several years for them to turn a profit.

5. **Institutional Ownership**

Ideally, you should look at the institutional ownership of every individual stock you own. I was at a stock investor's conference a few years ago, where

I met one of the world's top investors, and author of many stock investing books. I asked him how much institutional ownership of a stock he thinks is ideal. He seemed a bit caught off guard by my question, and didn't have an immediate answer, before responding "some but not much." That is not a helpful answer. I assume he means 50%? In my opinion, a 50/50 split, or as close as possible to that, is ideal between institutional and retail ownership. Frankly though, you are rarely going to find that perfect split. A good example of a company that has a lot of institutional ownership is the popular burger joint Jack in the Box (ticker: JACK). Their stock has almost 100% institutional ownership. This is great if all the large institutions and funds are buying, but not so great if they all decide to sell at one time. If you want to see what a stock chart looks like with an extremely large percentage of institutional ownership, pull up Jack In The Box's stock chart. It will make you dizzy because it looks like a roller coaster, with wild up and down price swings.

6. **Gross Margin**

The gross margin is the percentage of a company's revenue that is greater than its cost of goods sold (COGS). The gross margin percentage is another way for investors to determine whether a company is a good investment. It can also help companies understand whether there are any inefficiencies within their business, and shine a light on things they could do to cut costs and increase profits. Gross margin is expressed as a percentage, and the higher the number the better. If the gross margin is trending down and is very low, then that might be considered 'gross.' This might be a mental way for you to remember gross margin.

A company's gross margin is calculated by subtracting the cost of goods sold from the company's revenue. Then divide that figure by the total revenue and multiply it by 100 to get the gross margin. For example, if the ratio is calculated to be 60%, that means for every dollar of revenue a company generates, $.60 is retained while $.40 is attributed to the cost of goods sold. A business tries to have as high a gross margin as possible, so it can have more cash flow to pay for indirect operating costs.

While gross margin remains an important metric for businesses to track, it provides an incomplete picture in isolation. The cost of goods sold is only the direct cost associated with producing goods, including both direct labor costs, and any costs of materials used in producing or manufacturing a company's products. The gross margin only considers the cost of goods sold and does not include other operating expenses such as rent, utilities, salaries, and marketing costs. As a result, the gross margin does not provide a complete picture of the company's profitability.

Once we calculate the gross margin how do we tell if it is a 'good' gross margin percentage? The gross margin varies by industry. Service-based industries tend to have higher gross margins, because they do not have a large COGS. The gross margin for manufacturing companies will be lower because they have a larger COGS. A bank, for example, might have a gross margin of 99%, while for an automobile manufacturer it might be 10%. The best method for determining a good gross profit margin involves comparing your percentages to sector averages. You can do an internet search to find gross margins by industry, and then compare your company's gross margins to those industry averages.

7. **Short Float**

You likely haven't heard about short float before, especially if you're new to investing, but it has become important, and something you should be aware of. Actually, in my opinion, it's kind of sad that I even have to write about short float, but it's a topic that most were not taught in college or graduate school finance classes.

Financial institutions short stocks to hedge against a stock market crash. This strategy can pave the way for crazy moves in those shorted stocks, like GameStop in 2021. GameStop brought short selling to prominence back then. Short interest percentage is the only number you need, and it's simply the number of shares shorted divided by the total float of the stock, and multiplied by 100. I find it best and most accurate to get this percentage number from the website Finviz. Lately, it's been the only number I trust. It is important to note that these numbers are only refreshed twice a month, usually on the first and the 15th. It is always good to cross check the short float numbers on the various free financial websites. Just look for the metric called short float percentage. I would say that short float should not be a very large part of your stock investing thesis. In my opinion it is something you should just "take a peek at." It is a 'nice to have,' since a short squeeze like GameStop could boost your stock dramatically in a very short amount of time. Short float is really only important as a measure of sentiment. People that short a stock must pay interest on the borrowed shares. If the short float is high, you know that people remain committed to their belief that the price will go lower. Be on the lookout for stocks that have high short interest and are making new highs. There is generally a higher likelihood that the stock will 'squeeze.' Even more so if the stock has a low float.

8. **Beta**

Beta is explained in great detail in Chapter 19, but, briefly, beta denotes volatility of a stock compared to the overall market. The beta of the S&P 500 Index is 1. This index is the benchmark that every stock can be compared to. I always look at the beta of any stock I'm looking to buy. This gives a sense of the amount of turbulence you might be subjecting yourself to while owning the stock.

9. **Long Term Debt**

Just like debt in your personal life, it is always a good idea to see how much debt a company you own, or are considering investing in, is carrying. I believe it is wise to examine the balance sheet of a company, since debt is often involved when a business fails. Debt of a company can give you a clue to the amount of a company's risk exposure. Often when you read about a business failing, debt is involved. Debt and other liabilities pose a risk for a company when it cannot fulfill their obligations, either with free cash flow or by raising capital at an attractive price. If things get really bad, lenders can force a company to raise capital at a distressed stock price, permanently diluting shareholders.

When considering a company's debt levels, you need to look at their cash as well, as they go hand in hand. Don't forget about a company's earnings and profits either, because that is where the cash to pay off debts comes from. A company can usually only pay off debt with cold hard cash. Cash means a company can reduce its debt whenever it wants to. An easy way to quickly examine a company's debt is to look at its long-term debt ratio. I use the free portion of the website Finviz to find this ratio. Go to that website, enter your stock ticker, then look at the ratio called long term debt to equity, which is expressed as a percentage. The long-term debt-to-total-assets ratio is a measurement representing the percentage of a corporation's assets financed with long-term debt. A long-term debt ratio of 0.5 or less is generally considered good. You will find that if you look at the long-term debt ratio of a large, established company like Google that has a lot of cash and very little debt, it will be extremely small. I will warn that analyzing the debt of a company can get complex, so if you want to learn more about it, I would suggest going to the website Investopedia, or other financial websites that explain it in greater detail.

10. **Price To Sales (P/S) Ratio**

The price-to-sales ratio, abbreviated as P/S ratio, is a formula used to measure the total value that investors place on the company in comparison to the total revenue generated by the business. This is a ratio that I often use when analyzing a stock. It is a simple gauge of a company's market valuation based on its annual sales. I find it easiest, and most accurate, to get this ratio from the website Finviz, but it's fairly easy to calculate it yourself. I often do the calculation of it in my head very quickly, by just looking at two numbers. Divide the total market capitalization of the company by the annual sales. Remember to make sure both are in the same unit of measure (millions or billions, for example). For example, if a stock has a total market capitalization of $60 billion (you can get this market capitalization directly from the Yahoo Finance website) and total annual revenue of $30 billion, you simply divide 60 by 30 and get a P/S ratio of 2.0. I put a good amount of weight into the P/S ratio, as I think it helps show if a company's stock price has a crazy over-valuation. In general, a high P/S ratio may suggest that the stock is overvalued, whereas a lower ratio could imply that the stock is undervalued. It is important to note where the company is in its life cycle. Companies that are growing fast usually have a higher P/S ratio because people expect them to have higher sales and make more money in the future. The P/S ratio does have some limitations though, as it does not provide any information on the profitability of the company. Hence, it is important for investors to look at the P/S ratio along with other financial ratios, not just individually.

CHAPTER 9
ETFs

If people never bought an individual stock again, I don't think any financial advisor would say there was anything wrong with that premise. Retail investors, like us, account for only a small percentage of the ownership of stocks. Studies show roughly 80% of equity market capitalization is held by institutions (i.e.-pension funds, mutual funds, foreign investments, ...etc.) Compare this to 1950, when about 8% of the value of shares traded on U.S. markets was owned by institutions. Financial institutions of today mostly buy indexes and ETFs. ETFs, or exchange-traded funds, are exactly as the name implies: funds that trade on exchanges, generally tracking a specific index. These institutions that offer and manage the ETFs have sophisticated computer algorithms, artificial intelligence software, and highly qualified traders that do this for a living, so it is very difficult to try to beat them on your own. Institutional investors have a long-term outlook, whereas many individual investors lack a clearly defined target holding period. Because their purchases are preceded by a thorough analysis, sometimes lasting years, large financial institutions cannot easily jump from one stock to another. The average investor cannot consistently beat the returns of ETFs and index funds. These large financial institutions have better data, better technology, and more skilled managers. This is why I allocate a portion of my portfolio to ETFs. Another positive is that competition amongst these institutions has driven down costs and management fees, which is great for investors.

What makes ETFs appealing is their low cost and low fees. This is possible because in many cases, there is no active fund manager, as some ETFs are considered a passive form of investing. It is very difficult for the active investor to beat the sophistication and returns of ETFs. Trying to beat the market becomes a vicious cycle; if you buy individual stocks on your own and try to beat the returns of ETFs, then you risk missing out on living and enjoying your life in pursuit of the holy grail of outperformance. Plus, you could end up losing your money if you are not skilled at picking individual stocks.

Some may invest in ETFs, as opposed to individual stocks, in sectors they like that are otherwise complex and risky industries. An example of this is solar power, or cybersecurity, both of which have plenty of ETFs. I can see how ETFs can be confusing to investors. People, myself included, think all ETFs are passive, meaning, there is no active portfolio manager. This is the main reason people choose ETFs, because costs are low. However, there are actually many actively managed ETFs, as well.

ETFs used to be synonymous with passive investing, but lately, the actively managed ETFs' share of the U.S. ETF market has more than quadrupled, from just over 2.0% to 8.5%. An actively managed ETF features many of the same benefits of a traditional exchange-traded fund, but with a fund manager that can adapt the fund to changing market conditions. The underlying concept behind an actively managed ETF is that a portfolio manager adjusts the investments within the fund as desired, while not being subject to the set rules of tracking an index, like a passively managed ETF attempts to do.

The math behind index funds and their historical performance has been proven to work. Index funds keep you from doing potentially damaging things you might do if you were in charge of picking individual stocks yourself, then figuring out when to buy and sell them. I compare this to keeping the flowers, and pulling the weeds. When a company is no longer suitable for inclusion in a particular index, which could be for a multitude of reasons, it will be removed like weeds. Index funds seem to be the ultimate "set it and forget it" investment. They 'self-cleanse' themselves with periodic rebalancing. Index rebalancing is the periodic adjustment of an index's asset weights to ensure it accurately reflects its purpose. Because the 500 stocks in the S&P's flagship index fluctuate in value over time, that means some new companies will be added to the index periodically, while others are removed, a process known as index rebalancing. The S&P 500 rebalances on a quarterly basis, as does the Dow Jones and the Nasdaq 100 Index, two other highly relevant indexes.

One of the main benefits of some ETFs is their low costs and low fees. Two of the most popular passively managed ETFs are the Vanguard VOO and the Invesco QQQ. Their annual fees are .03% and .20%, respectively. Both are passively managed, and happen to be my two favorites. I dollar cost average, commonly known as DCA, into my retirement plan at work into these two index funds. Often, these two passive index funds outperform the return in the portfolio of individual stocks I actively manage. I choose to invest mostly in these two, and we discuss in the rest of this chapter the reasons why, which are mostly related to risk and reward, and of course annual management fees and costs.

Currently, there are approximately 3,243 ETFs, and that is just in the United States. Not surprisingly, there has been a massive increase from just 123 in 2003. Many attribute the large increase to the fact that creators of these active ETFs, and to an extent the passive ETFs, make a lot of money for themselves from managing them. Several of the more popular actively managed ETFs charge annual expense fees averaging around .75%, which is significantly higher than the annual expense fees of VOO and QQQ, both below .20%. Even Buffett's Berkshire Hathaway has very low management fees. Management and expense fees that some funds charge can, over time, significantly reduce your overall returns in their funds. We will examine in the rest of this chapter if some popular, and very low-cost ETFs, are the right place to possibly park your money, instead of some high-flying ETFs that charge considerably higher annual management and expense fees.

An analysis of passive ETF returns vs actively managed Berkshire Hathaway

At Berkshire Hathaway's 2021 shareholders meeting, Warren Buffett stated, frankly, "I do not think the average person can pick stocks." Instead, he has repeatedly said that most people should invest their money in a low-cost, S&P 500 Index fund. In fact, he has included that recommendation in his will. "One bequest provides that cash will be delivered to a trustee for my wife's benefit," he wrote in his 2013 letter to Berkshire shareholders. "My advice to the trustee could not be simpler: Put 10% of the cash in short-term government bonds and 90% in a very low-cost S&P 500 Index fund."

Let's do a comparison of returns over the last 24 years to see if Warren Buffett is right. We will analyze the returns of his own Berkshire Hathaway Fund against two of the most popular ETFs we have looked at, VOO and QQQ. The three have similarly low annual expense fees and similar risk profiles. Returns are approximate total returns, with dividends reinvested.

TIME PERIOD 2000 – 2024, showing total returns with dividends reinvested

Berkshire Hathaway +1,100%

S&P 500 Index +529%

Invesco QQQ +496%

TIME PERIOD 2014 – 2024, showing total returns with dividends reinvested

Berkshire Hathaway +270%

S&P 500 Index +267%

Invesco QQQ +505%

CONCLUSIONS

Passively managed index funds seem like a nice, low-cost way to get some good returns, without enduring much pain. It is easy to see why they are so popular. We discussed, at length, the two most popular ETFs, VOO and QQQ. Warren Buffett's returns do well over the last quarter century when compared to the popular indexes. The only time he got trounced was the last ten-year timeframe against the QQQs, but over the last twenty-four-year period he fared much better, comparatively. However, Buffett didn't get beat *that* bad. The QQQs outperformed almost every other fund over the past ten years. Keep in mind, too, that the QQQs have a lot more volatility than Berkshire Hathaway's fund.

CHAPTER 10
DIVIDENDS

In my opinion, dividends are one of the greatest things in the stock investing world. If you don't believe me, then at least listen to Warren Buffett because he says the same thing. Just look at Buffett's stock portfolio over the years, and even his current stock portfolio. It is loaded with dividend stocks.

Dividends are money that a company is giving you. Why would companies want to give you money and even pay dividends? Because they want to attract investors and keep you a happy shareholder. It also demonstrates financial strength and provides underlying support for the stock price. Remember with dividends that companies are *paying you* to keep your money with them. Lately, there is even more focus on dividends as compared to the extremely low rate of return on bonds; thus, dividends can be looked upon as providing a much better return than bonds. Keep in mind, though, that you must report and pay tax on any dividends received during the year, even if you do not take the cash and reinvest the dividends into more company shares.

Some investors, including many prominent ones, only buy stocks that pay a dividend. They view a stock that doesn't pay a dividend as pure speculation and not an investment, as it doesn't pay you anything and there is no guarantee the stock will go up. Companies that are loyal to their stock buyers reward them with increasing dividends. During the pandemic of 2020 companies streamlined, and big, solid companies had good free cash flow, so dividends were one way they can return money to their shareholders. Dividend stocks can produce good results with significantly less volatility than ones that do not pay a dividend. To be clear, this is not true of all dividend stocks, but I think many. Stocks of many dividend-paying companies can crash and burn just like any stock. However, dividend stocks may lag on the way up, but they also tend to hold up better when the market goes down. When you use your dividend earnings to purchase additional shares of company stock, you'll earn more money, because every share you purchase earns its own regular dividend payout. This compounding strategy benefits from the power of exponential growth: your original investment generates a certain return that can be reinvested to produce greater returns, and those returns can be reinvested, and so on. Further, companies that pay dividends are typically stable and their share price usually increases over time so you also get an additional return on your investment when share prices hopefully increase. The other benefit you get by owning dividend stocks and reinvesting the dividends is that even when their stock price is falling it means you can buy more shares when you reinvest because of the stock price being lower. Over the long-term, and assuming the stock price eventually goes higher, you can benefit greatly because you can accumulate more shares at the lower stock price.

People often forget that dividends can act as a hedge against inflation, the overall rise in prices of goods and services. For an investor to realize a net gain from an investment, the investment must first provide enough of a return to overcome the loss of purchasing power that results from inflation. The good news is that dividends can preserve your purchasing power, as dividend yields can typically outpace inflation. As I write this, inflation is quite high, as are interest rates. Right now, I'm getting about 5.25% annual interest, risk-free, on Certificates of Deposit (CDs). This is higher than most of the yields I am earning on my dividend stocks. It won't stay like this for long. At some point dividend stocks will be more attractive, as interest rates will go down, and theoretically the yield that dividend stocks pay will be higher than bank savings rates.

Remember, though, companies can start or stop paying dividends at any time, so it is important not to take false security from dividend stocks. You can say all you want about dividend stocks, but when bad things happen in the world they still generally perform well and at least pay you something, that something being their dividend. I have a large part of my stock portfolio in dividend paying stocks. You can invest in solid oil companies or insurance companies, for example, that consistently pay a dividend. If you are looking to live off part of your dividends in retirement, you need preservation of capital. Also, I use the automatic Dividend Reinvestment Plan, DRIP, in my brokerage account. A DRIP is an arrangement that allows shareholders to automatically reinvest a stock's cash dividends into additional or fractional shares of the underlying company.

Some investors only look for a company's ability to generate free cash flow, which are companies that pay dividends. Some may perceive these dividend paying companies as boring, but they are typically financially stable. People cannot afford to gamble with their retirement.

Investing in dividends stocks, I believe, is so important that I want to give a sports analogy to make the point of investing in dividend stocks more relatable. I love golf, and have played since college. A few years back I was fortunate enough to have a private golf lesson with a PGA professional golfer. He was on the PGA Senior Tour and operated out of a golf course right near where I live here in New Jersey. He was chatting with me before our lesson officially began, and told me he had just played in a golf tournament the prior weekend with Jack Nicklaus and Tom Watson. At the driving range, he told me to hit some balls so he could quickly assess my golf swing. I hit five or six in a row straight and far. I remember being very proud of myself, and turning to him to ask, "Didn't that look great?" He responded by saying that it looked pretty good, but reminded me that I had to do that about sixty-five more times in a row to be considered just an average *par* golfer. Consistency is the name of the game here. Just like you need a consistent golf swing to stay straight on the golf course, consider consistent dividend stocks the backbone of any stock portfolio.

In stock investing, the only thing that might be better than dividend stocks are dividend growth stocks. You might be surprised to know this, but Microsoft, Apple, and Google pay their shareholders a dividend. Microsoft and Apple have been paying a dividend for many years, but Google just recently decided to pay one as well. Keep in mind, too, that these stocks have a rather low dividend yield. But don't let that turn you off, because the overall returns of these dividend growth stocks can compound greatly over long periods of time. My favorite dividend growth stock that I own is Texas Roadhouse (ticker: TXRH) and we will be discussing their returns in a later chapter. By the way, I also would not forget that one of the best investments out there, the S&P500 Index ETFs (Exchange Traded Funds like ticker VOO) also pay a dividend. It's not much of a yield, but adds up over time. I found the website *ofdollarsanddata* that has a great free S&P 500 historical return calculator. You can go on that website and see results with dividends reinvested, as well. The calculator even factors in inflation adjusted returns.

Another opinion that some have regarding dividend investing, is that if you are younger, consider putting a larger percentage of your portfolio into growth (maybe technology stocks) and/or dividend growth stocks. Then, as you get closer to retirement age you can always put a much larger percentage of your portfolio into what may be considered less risky dividend-only stocks, if you need to live on the dividend. This is just opinion, and you need to do your own research on how much of a percentage of your portfolio you want to keep in dividend stocks. It is not an easy allocation to decide, and if you are unsure you might want to seek the services of a paid investment advisor.

CHAPTER 11
DIVERSIFICATION

Y ou can own eighty stocks, but if they are all in the same industry, you are not diversified. Diversification is critically important to your stock portfolio, as it can weatherproof it in case of market downturns. You have insurance on your life, car, and home, but how about your $1 million stock portfolio? If you are going to go it alone and try to build your own portfolio of individual stocks, then diversification is your insurance policy. By diversification, I mean not only the number of stocks you own, but also the industry and sector those stocks are in.

Ray Dalio, a billionaire money manager, has spoken about the importance of diversification. Dalio even goes as far to call it the 'Holy Grail' of investing. How many stocks should you own for a diversified portfolio? Experts say that 12-15 stocks spread amongst different sectors is the way to go. Personally, I follow this rule and I own right around 15 individual stocks in my portfolio. It has been studied those additional stocks after around 15 provide little additional diversification benefit. The chart below, based on data from the classic book *A Random Walk Down Wall Street* by Burton Malkiel, shows how further increase in the number of holdings does not produce any significant further risk reduction. The chart shows total portfolio risk as a function of number of stocks held, which appear on the X axis. So, there appears to be a sort of 'sweet spot' for the number of stocks you should own.

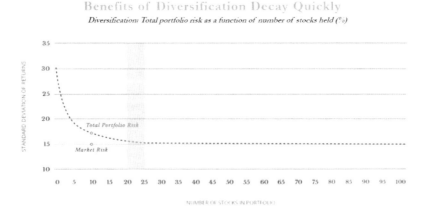

In fact, having too many stocks could cause what some have termed "di-worseification." Peter Lynch says having too many stocks is like having too many children, as you must 'babysit' each stock. Peter Lynch is famous for saying "The best stock to buy is the one you already own." Lynch says to buy something you're happy to own and buy more when opportunities allow. Also, the general rule is that you do not allocate more than 5% of your stock portfolio to any one stock. Diversification can help to obtain reasonable returns, while minimizing risk. Diversification is great, but seems its benefits are realized with far fewer stocks that most people realize.

You may know people that say they only own two or three stocks. I know a few myself that mostly own Tesla stock and Bitcoin. I think those that say they only own two stocks are lying. Almost everyone's investments are diversified, in some capacity. Someone might say they own two stocks, but zoom out and look at that person's overall portfolio and life. They likely have money in cash, CDs, dividend stocks, ETFs, REITs, or hard real estate as well, and they might even own some Bitcoin. So, I would always be cautious when someone tells you they are not diversified with their stock investments.

Let's examine one person that has been highly successful in the stock market by not diversifying. Warren Buffett, the head of **Berkshire Hathaway**. More than 43% of Warren Buffett-led Berkshire Hathaway's nearly $400 billion portfolio is invested in only one stock: Apple (ticker: $AAPL) You could say it is the 'Apple' of Buffett's eye. Buffett is one of the rare exceptions where concentration has actually worked. Then again, he is Warren Buffett. "I would say for anyone … who really knows the businesses they have gone into, six [stocks] is plenty," Buffett says, adding that "very few people have gotten rich on their seventh-best idea." Keep in mind, though, most of us are not nearly as smart an investor as Buffett, who started buying Apple stock in 2016 when its p/e ratio was only around 10. So, its valuation at the time was historically low. It is important to note that Buffett only holds around 44 individual stocks in his Berkshire Hathaway portfolio. Apple stock has organically grown to be his largest holding, but he does own many other stocks.

You must figure out the number of stocks you want to own that works for your personal situation. If you recall back to the Introduction chapter, where I documented my experiences with some investors that I have encountered throughout my life. The ones I know that lost the most money in stocks, even into the millions of dollars, were not diversified enough. On the flip side, you don't want to own so many stocks that you have your own 'mini' index fund. Personally, if I had to err on the side of caution, I would rather be a little more diversified than not.

Asset Allocation

Very simply, asset allocation refers to the overall mixture of stocks, bonds, cryptocurrencies, real estate, and other asset classes in your portfolio, and how much of your money is invested in each one. Asset allocation (or the overall composition of your portfolio) is more important than any individual stock within it. While stocks run hot or cold, the correct asset allocation keeps you steered in the right direction for the long term. Asset allocation matters because it aims to balance risk in your portfolio. Asset classes typically fall into three broad categories: stocks, bonds, and cash. Anything outside these three categories (for example: real estate, art, collectibles, cryptocurrencies, etc.) is often referred to as alternative assets. Asset allocation is a personal decision that varies by individual and can depend on various factors, including age, financial targets, and appetite for risk. Investment management company The Vanguard Group relates asset allocation in your stock portfolio in the same way to where you live. If, for example, you move to San Diego, your overall weather will be very similar to that of someone living in Los Angeles. It won't matter very much which of those cities you choose or what month you move there, what's important is that you're living in Southern California and not New England.

Rebalancing

How do you deal with adversity? What will you do when there is a huge market correction? Keep in mind I said *when* not *if*. You should always be mentally prepared to lose half or even all your money in the stock market. We will discuss what to do if you get punched in the face, like if the stock market crashes or there is a global pandemic. Rebalancing is how you can fight your portfolio back to profitability.

Many financial experts, including Warren Buffett, advise investors to hold a stock forever if you can. While that may be good advice and what I would normally practice, it is not always a reality and, in some cases, could cause you to lose a lot of money. At certain times you may need to reallocate your portfolio, as an emergency may cause you to rethink your investments. After the pandemic stock market crash in March 2020, I would not have made as much money on the rebound if I just stayed the course and did not touch or move out of the investments in my stock portfolio. People that tell you to never sell a stock are not totally correct all the time. I am a perfect example. After the stock market crash in March 2020, if I had done absolutely nothing and stayed the course in my stock investments, I would have done just *ok*. Soon after the crash, the stock market had monumental gains for the next twelve months or so. Prior to the crash I had a fairly large percentage of my retirement portfolio invested in international stocks, as they were providing me high returns. After the crash, the international mutual fund I was invested in, and that sector in general, did not do well at all. Had I not reallocated my port-folio to the technology mutual funds I rebalanced my money into I would not have earned nearly as much money on the market rebound.

Rebalancing is the process of realigning the weightings of a portfolio of assets. Rebalancing involves periodically buying or selling assets in a portfolio to maintain an original or desired level of asset allocation or risk. Markets and economies change, and individual businesses change. A holding that was attractive ten years ago may no longer seem as attractive in the current market. Investors should be looking at their investments twice a year; this includes your 401k or IRA. The idea of "set it and forget it" is not totally correct. You will likely need to rotate your individual stock holdings at some point.

CHAPTER 12

MOST STOCKS ARE BAD INVESTMENTS

The stock markets have increased dramatically the past fifteen years, mostly due to low interest rates and government stimulus. It seems many of us have gotten spoiled with 20% and up stock returns some years. We will explore how historically difficult it has been to achieve those high returns, and that it may have raised the bar a bit too much.

My friends invest heavily in commercial real estate, and sometimes they ask me to invest with them. They show me reports of annual returns of around 8% on prospective commercial real estate properties. I always thought growing up, and for a large part of my life, that 8% was a great return on an investment, until the last couple of years. It seems like in today's world that the bar has been raised, and that many investors today are not very happy with *only*, for example, an 8% annual return. Many people now look at that as an 'average' rate of return, and wonder how you could be satisfied with such a low annual return. Ironically, this was even in an interest rate environment back in 2020-2021 when interest rates hovered near zero; so, in theory, the bar should have been extremely low.

I believe that investors today have a distorted view of what is a good rate of return. Investors need to be realistic, and keep in the back of their minds that it is difficult to consistently get yearly returns of greater than 15%, or even 10% for that matter, in the stock market. You might appreciate, and long for, an 8% return if, for example, the U.S. economy goes into a recession and the stock market has several years in a row of negative returns.

We have been in a ten year or so bull market run, and the S&P 500 has returned higher than its normal returns over that time, but one cannot expect this to last forever. At the time of writing, the U.S. economy is flush with cash from government stimulus money from the global pandemic. As a result, the bar for investor expectations for returns has been raised higher. Investors have been satisfied with an 8% stock market return in the past. About forty years ago you could easily have earned this much just on your savings account at your bank. The decade from 2011 through 2020, for example, has been great for stocks. The average stock market return during that time period was around 13.9% annually for the **S&P 500 (note: this return is before inflation).** Now, it seems, people are not satisfied with a 13% S&P 500 return, as a lot of investors think they can beat it. Well, as you have read so far in this book, this is difficult to accomplish.

It's appropriate that I put this chapter right after the last chapter on diversification, as it reinforces the point of being diversified.

Most Stocks Are Bad Investments

Research by Professor Hendrik Bessembinder, and others, at Arizona State University's W. P. Carey School of Business, evaluated lifetime returns for every U.S. common stock traded on the New York, American, and Nasdaq stock exchanges from 1926 through 2017. Bessembinder's groundbreaking research has been covered extensively in major news outlets. The key findings of this important study are below (sources: see footnotes at end of this chapter):

> **Finding 1:** 58% of stocks failed to beat Treasury bill returns over time. Treasury bills are short-term investments backed by the U.S. Treasury, making them a safe place to hold your cash and earn a modest interest rate. These investments are typically for one year or less, and you purchase them at a discount. At maturity, you receive the face value, letting you earn a return. For a risk-averse investor, T-bills offer steady, albeit typically low, returns and are useful for preserving capital and maintaining liquidity. However, their low-risk nature also means they generally provide lower yields compared to other investments, and potentially will not keep pace with inflation over time.

Finding 2: 38% of stocks beat Treasury bill returns by just moderate amounts.

Finding 3: Just over 4% of stocks are responsible for boosting the market's overall returns higher than those on Treasury bills. He found that the largest returns came from very few stocks overall – just 86 stocks accounted for most of the wealth creation over the last 90 years of the study. Take note, his report studied over 20,000 publicly-listed common stocks.

The following are some excerpts from a back-and-forth Q&A from an October 29, 2020 interview given by Bessembinder with international asset manager firm Robeco:

Can you give us a sense of how the composition of wealth builders has changed over time?

"While I have not investigated this issue systematically, it is clear that a small group of technology-related stocks, such as Apple, Amazon, Alphabet and Facebook, are responsible for a substantial portion of the stock market's recent wealth creation, particularly in recent years. In a new study, I provide an update on this. On the other hand, thousands of technology stocks have delivered disappointing returns in the long run as well, so the implication is not as simple as; just buy technology stocks."

You make an interesting observation that the degree of wealth concentration has actually increased over the last 25 years. What do you think is driving that?

"The short answer is that I do not know. But it may be the case that the internet-based economy has allowed for more 'winner-take-all' outcomes in certain industries."

How do you see the skewness of returns evolving over the next five to ten years?

"I see no reason to think that the future will be markedly different from the past. Stated differently, I am confident that a relatively small proportion of stocks will be responsible for a large share of market performance over the next decade. Which stocks that will be is, of course, a much harder question to answer."

In summary, the results of this extensive study reinforce the desirability of having a well-diversified portfolio, which increases the chances that some of your stocks will be big winners. Bessembinder himself even says that "a poorly diversified portfolio has a less than 50% chance of beating a diversified portfolio."

The Hard Truth About Stock Investing

It is a tough game over any extended time period to try to beat the returns of the S&P 500 Index by picking individual stocks. Warren Buffett has even had a bad decade or two. According to market research firm DataTrek, Warren Buffett's Berkshire

Hathaway has *underperformed* the QQQ Tech Index from a 20-year period beginning in 2003. It's not a matter of Warren Buffett underperforming, it is that the technology stocks alone that make up the QQQ Index have outperformed all the other stocks, even in their own index.

It might be a good idea to set realistic expectations when it comes to stock investing. The S&P 500 has historically generated an average annual return of between 8% and 15%. Only a handful of some of the most successful investors in history have ever significantly exceeded those returns over a period of ten or more years. Keep in mind, when the stock market undergoes a large correction, which it inevitably will, that an 8% return might look pretty attractive. When a market correction happens, you will be happy your investments are diversified, which reinforces what we just learned in this chapter and the last chapter.

Now is a good time to bring up a quote from Bill Parcells that may help you think when you're picking stocks and building out your stock portfolio. Bill Parcells is one of the best coaches in NFL history, and along the way he proved to be incredibly quotable. Parcells said: "It's not who has the best team, it's which team plays the best." This has parallels to stocks, and building your stock portfolio. Your roster, or stock portfolio, can be loaded with star names, but that doesn't mean it will perform well. Upcoming chapter twenty-four, called Opportunity Cost, discusses in detail some high-quality, profitable companies whose stocks don't necessarily perform that well.

Footnotes

Bessembinder, H., 2020. "Wealth Creation in the U.S. Public Stock Markets 1926 to 2019", working paper.

Bessembinder, H., 2020. "Extreme Stock Market Performers, Part I: Expect Some Drawdowns", working paper.

Bessembinder, H., 2020. "Extreme Stock Market Performers, Part II: Do Technology Stocks Dominate?", working paper.

Bessembinder, H., 2020. "Extreme Stock Market Performers, Part III: What are their Observable Characteristics?", working paper.

Bessembinder, H., 2020. "Extreme Stock Market Performers, Part IV: Can Observable Characteristics Forecast Outcomes?", working paper.

CHAPTER 13
PORTFOLIO CASH

You need to have cash to buy stocks, as you can't purchase stocks with a credit card. First, do not mix up or lump together portfolio cash and the cash you hold in bank accounts as an emergency fund. They are different. For the purposes of this chapter, we will be talking about portfolio cash. Your portfolio cash is the amount of money you have available to purchase investments, for example, like stocks.

Mark Cuban is an American billionaire entrepreneur, television personality, and investor. He has stated in interviews that he is usually skeptical of the stock market, and advises to always keep a lot of cash on the sidelines. In an exclusive interview with Young Money, a personal finance education and media company, Cuban offered this general investing advice and then followed the statement by saying, "The idiots that tell you to put your money in the market because eventually it will go up need to tell you that because they are trying to sell you something." Rather than put all your eggs in the stock market, Cuban encourages keeping some money in a savings account for a rainy day, so you're protected if something goes wrong. According to Cuban, the purpose of saving money isn't to prepare for retirement. It's so that you always have cash on hand when you need it. Having investments is one thing, but think what would happen if you really needed money and it was all tied up in things you never sell. Cuban states that the "best place to invest is to pay off all your credit cards and burn them." Cuban says you should do this, because when you use your credit card, you know the return. For example, Cuban says that if you're paying 22% interest on your credit card and once you pay that down, you've just earned 22%. General advice would be if you're going to use your credit card, you should do so responsibly. For example, using your credit card to build a credit score means paying your credit card bills on time, as payment history is calculated in your credit score.

Additionally, Cuban says it is also good to have a lot of cash around for stock market crashes, in order to be able to purchase stocks cheaply. Keep in mind stock market crashes are usually followed by a rally, that's how things have historically played out. Mark Cuban is a billionaire, and I've never met a dumb billionaire in my life, and I've personally met two billionaires. Speaking for myself, in this case, I would tend to listen to Cuban.

What is the ideal level of portfolio cash you should keep on hand? It all comes down to a personal judgement decision based on what works for you. If I am doing well and have a good outlook for the stock market and economy, I may simply just not have enough cash to buy new stocks because most of my money will already be invested in the rising stock market.

Interest rates are a big factor too, and back in 2020-2021 when I wrote my first stock investing book **Night Trading**, interest rates were near zero. With extremely low interest rates my portfolio cash position was low, since I did not want to keep my portfolio cash earning near zero percent return at the bank. Back in the 2020-2021 low-interest rate environment, some were calling the stock market the new bank, or the new place to put your cash. With near zero interest rates back in 2020-2021 some people felt you would be better off investing in a S&P 500 Index fund. Fast forward to 2023-2024, a time with higher interest rates, I had almost 30% of my net worth in cash, because interest rates were high and I was easily earning 5%+ in certificates of deposit (CDs). You have to make your own decision regarding how much cash to have, based on your aversion to risk.

Emotions also play a factor in how much portfolio cash you plan on allocating, which ties in to how much risk you are willing take on. Emotions occupy a powerful position in making investment decisions, as they drive human behavior. Emotions play an important role when making decisions on investments, just like any business or other decisions that you are confronted with in life.

Many people will tell you the worst thing to be invested in is cash. However, if you are bad at picking stocks and investing, you might be better off keeping your money in cash, especially if interest rates are high and you can earn good money in CDs risk-free. I have seen many people lose a lot of money in stocks when, in retrospect, they would have been much better off in cash. If you don't know what you are doing investing in stocks, you might be better off in cash. And in an environment where banks are paying 5%, and even higher, risk-free interest rates, that may not be a bad idea.

CHAPTER 14
TAKE A GMBL

T he title of this chapter is not a misspelling of the word gamble. GMBL refers to the stock ticker of a company that we'll be discussing.

At any time, I usually like to be invested in one speculative, or 'spec,' stock in my portfolio. As the title of this chapter states, one could also call this "taking a gamble." That said, I would like to discuss a strategy and mindset that is critical to this chapter and, quite frankly, much of stock investing. It involves risk management and mindset. Here it is:

"Bet a little to possibly make a lot - NOT bet a lot to possibly make a lot."

I developed this idea, and I use it often with how I approach stock investing. The quote appears original to myself, as I've never seen it used before. It is an important mindset quote, I believe, for the fact that it gets to the heart of risk management. If you recall back to the Introduction of this book, where I mentioned investors I came across that lost a lot of money in the stock market. It seems they did not practice good risk management, as most of them lost large amounts of money because they invested too much in only one stock. Unfortunately for them, that one stock went down, and never went back up.

A perfect example of where this mindset could apply is Bitcoin, which is discussed in great detail in the next chapter. Even if you had invested an extremely small amount of money in Bitcoin many years ago it would be worth a lot today. Another example of my "bet a little" investing strategy is options trading. I also do some options trading, which is the epitome of "bet a little." However, this is not a book on options trading. There are many books and resources available on options trading.

I once read an article that recommended a stock traded on the Nasdaq exchange called Esports Entertainment Group. The ticker symbol was appropriately GMBL, which has to be one of the coolest stock tickers ever. But what exactly is esports? Esports is a form of competitive video gaming, which is watched and appreciated as a spectator event. Even before the 2020 pandemic, esports and competitive gaming had been experiencing strong growth. The growth in spectator competitive gaming has also given rise to esports betting and wagering. I do not know anything about video games nor do I even play them, but I was aware enough to know at the time that video gaming was a hot and growing sector. And the company had just inked a deal with an NFL football team, and were looking to strike partnerships with other professional sports teams. That sealed it for me, and without overthinking it, I took a gamble on GMBL.

Actually, it would have been near impossible to do any quality research at all on the company, because at the time they were just recently publicly traded and they had not reported any revenue. Like any new business, they could go out of business before they even made a profit. This is the case for a lot of young technology companies. I don't remember the exact price I bought GMBL stock, but as I recall it was around $7. Fortunately, a few months later, the stock actually doubled in price, and soon after even briefly tripled. Luckily, I sold all my stock in the company relatively quickly, and was able to take profits. In this particular case, I was very happy I took the GMBL.

Eventually, this stock did end up coming back down to almost my initial purchase price. The company, and its stock price, eventually 'crashed and burned.' Esports Entertainment (GMBL) stock eventually voluntarily delisted from the Nasdaq stock exchange and switched its shares to the OTC exchange. The stock is a true 'penny stock' now, last trading at just 30 cents per share. My GMBL trade was simply that; a trade. I had no plans to marry the stock. I simply took advantage of what was in front of me at the time. You could say I took a GMBL.

Now, fast forward to the time of this writing in July 2024. I purchased a stock I had prior traded and already knew a lot about. That company is MicroStrategy (ticker: MSTR). MicroStrategy Incorporated is an American company that provides business intelligence (BI), mobile software, and cloud-based services. They also are involved with artificial intelligence, so I found that interesting about them. By the way, they are also a company that owns a large amount of Bitcoin – many billions of dollars' worth. The fact that I already understand and invest in Bitcoin, drew me into investing in MicroStrategy. As the price of Bitcoin has been rising over the last several years, so too has MicroStrategy's share price. There are a couple reasons many would look at MicroStrategy as a gamble. First, their stock is rather expensive on a per share price basis. Second, they invest a lot of their money into Bitcoin, which for that reason alone many would view as risky. I purchased shares at around $1,200 per share, and just 3 weeks later the stock was at $1,800. By any standards, a 50% return in 3 weeks is good.

To summarize, this chapter showed a couple examples of sometimes taking a gamble in the stock market, and how it can pay off. The other point that was reinforced is when taking these gambles, you don't always need to invest a lot to make a large return. Remember: "Bet a little to possibly make a lot - NOT bet a lot to possibly make a lot."

CHAPTER 15
THE 'MAINSTREAMIFICATION' OF BITCOIN

As discussed in Chapter 4, we were living in a very low interest rate environment back in 2020-2021 when I wrote *Night Trading.* That led many to say "cash is trash." Like many, I was simply trying to find a safe, low-risk place to park some of my money and make a decent return. People were trying to find places to put their liquidity to use. They wanted to preserve their wealth and earn a good yield. Due to the near zero interest rate paid by banks back then, and the specter of inflation, leaving my cash in the bank was simply not an option at the time of that book writing.

I investigated investing in gold. I think gold is a good investment and over long periods of time has provided a decent rate of return. The price of gold often does not move much over long periods, even five to ten years, but I simply do not have the patience to invest in gold. Also, gold does not pay a dividend (unless you buy a gold stock such as Barrick Gold), and neither does Bitcoin. Investing in gold will likely not make you wealthy, but that isn't the purpose of gold. Gold could prevent you from losing a lot of your money and preserve your wealth.

I got to thinking, and came across an investment that had been staring everyone in the face for many years: Bitcoin. Bitcoin and other cryptocurrencies (hereafter in this chapter referred to as crypto) are digital money. There is no physical coin or bill, it is all online. Bitcoin is often compared to gold. Bitcoin was made from scratch. Time and energy went into mining Bitcoin and running the Bitcoin network. It costs almost nothing for the Federal Reserve to literally print more money. There is barely any time and energy put into that, other than firing up a printing press and debasing the U.S. dollar even more.

Keep in mind, no one made gold, we found gold. And, if there is more of a demand for gold, miners will just mine more gold. Remember, too, that banks generally want to hoard all the gold. Central banks worldwide actively accumulate gold to diversify their reserves and reduce dependency on the US dollar. These foreign countries aim to hedge against currency depreciation and geopolitical risks.

Bitcoin is the biggest platform of all the cryptos and has the most market capitalization. Bitcoin is very liquid. Physical real estate, in comparison, is not very liquid. Also, you can buy fractional shares of Bitcoin and other cryptos. Regarding risk, many think Bitcoin is high risk. However, is it really that risky? It's been around a long time and has been one of the best-performing assets in the world over the last ten years. The crypto coin is just a representation of all the technology behind it.

Let's look at some of the differences between crypto and stocks. There are traditional ways to attempt to value a stock, like earnings per share (EPS), book value, P/E ratio, etc. This is called fundamental stock analysis and works well for most people, including myself. However, with crypto it is more difficult to value because it seems all its value is purely behavioral, worth only what people think it is worth. Does this sound like what is printed on the money in your wallet? Think of the saying "In God We Trust" written on U.S currency bills and coins. It seems U.S. currency and Bitcoin both have that 'trust factor' backing it. The gold standard is a monetary system in which the value of a country's currency is directly linked to gold. The U.S. went off the gold standard back in 1971.

Bitcoin is tribal, and crypto investing is mostly a behavioral-driven space that is still in price discovery mode. The limited supply of Bitcoin also helps to justify some of its value, as there are only 21 million total bitcoins. One thing I like is that Bitcoin, and many other cryptos, can be traded twenty-four hours a day. This is a distinct advantage, in my opinion, over stock investing. I also like the fact that you can easily convert one crypto to another crypto in just a few seconds with the click of a button. Occasionally, I convert my holdings from one crypto to another, sometimes at one-o-clock in the morning. As a comparison, you cannot just convert your Apple stock to

Tesla stock if you wanted. You would have to sell one and then buy the other.

Deciding between different types of investments always comes down to risk. This is where Bitcoin really shines, because over the last ten years investors have been rewarded for their risk – there has been almost no better total investment return than Bitcoin. I allocate 1-2% of my net worth into Bitcoin – this is in line with investment experts advising not to have more than 5% invested in any one asset.

To purchase Bitcoin and other crypto just find an exchange and setup a crypto wallet. There are several crypto exchanges out there. A word of warning – be prepared to pay a commission (usually 1.5%) to both buy and sell trades of crypto with many of the crypto exchanges. You could also simply buy Bitcoin through your PayPal account, but again commission rates do apply. It is likely that PayPal will offer many more cryptos for sale in the future. You could also buy stocks in companies that own a lot of Bitcoin. MicroStrategy (ticker: MSTR) would be one of those companies. MicroStrategy is a software company that is widely considered to be a Bitcoin proxy due to its massive holdings of Bitcoin.

Some people are not believers in Bitcoin, and there is a chance it could fail, although at this point that seems like an extremely small chance. I feel as Bitcoin becomes more mature the price will become less volatile. It may not go up as fast as it used to, but it could become a more stable store of value. Many naysayers of Bitcoin argue that you cannot buy anything with your Bitcoin, and you still must convert it to dollars eventually. That may be a valid argument, but I personally do not plan on selling much of my Bitcoin anytime soon.

In the future, you will likely start seeing traditional banks converge with the crypto market, which will be good news for both. Banks might hold all digital wallets. Banks could also offer blockchain support and even facilitate crypto transactions. One needs to look at the big picture with Bitcoin in that it is not just something here in the United States, but the entire world. Other countries with political uncertainty, may find Bitcoin even more appealing because it is not attached to any state.

Let's face it, Bitcoin and all cryptos are under threat from not only possible excessive government regulation, but also every central bank in every country in the world hoping to have its own digital currency. Central bank digital currencies, or CBDCs, are coming, and nothing will really stop them.

I think that all Bitcoin's shortcomings will actually put it in a better position than all other coins to survive long term, and retain its status as the crypto coin leader. Some say Bitcoin has slow transaction processing, and that it isn't realistic to be used as a mainstream method of payment. While true, I think Bitcoin stands the best chance to ultimately continue its reign as the coin with the largest market capitalization, and fully realize its status as digital gold. If Bitcoin ultimately accomplishes nothing else and becomes only a digital replacement for gold, then it could be worth much more than it is right now. At time of writing, the current market capitalization of Bitcoin is around $1 trillion dollars, while gold has a total market cap of roughly $15 trillion. There is still a long runway for Bitcoin to penetrate some of gold's market share.

I enjoy investing in Bitcoin. I think it is exciting, and also find my stock-picking skills can be applied to crypto. Crypto occasionally provides me a much-needed escape from the stock market. Sometimes, I will spend several days in a row, even a week, focused only on the crypto market, and not the stock market at all.

I view crypto as mostly a technology-driven space. Many say crypto has no intrinsic value. I am a technology person, and I feel that the value of crypto is mostly in its technology. It can also be a store of value for your money (mostly Bitcoin in my opinion), but I focus mostly on the technology, and if you read the whitepapers, you will see the technology of many cryptos is quite amazing.

From a technology standpoint, Bitcoin is just another protocol. A protocol, in regards to technology, is defined as a standardized set of rules for formatting and processing data. Examples of popular protocols that you might have heard of are: IP Internet protocol, TCPIP Transmission control protocol, SMTP Email transmission protocol, HTTP Web browser protocol, FTP file transfer protocol. Is BTC the money protocol? If you are looking to buy a particular crypto coin, I encourage you to do your research by going to their website and reading their whitepaper. I try not to focus too much on current price, since I am investing in an industry in its infancy.

Even if the entire crypto market corrects or crashes, much of the technology is not going to go away.

I am mostly a long-term investor. That said, I must invest in things that will also be around in the long term. You didn't need to be the *first* investor in Amazon or Google to make a large return on your investment, as you still could have made a lot of money if you invested in them years after they became established. Since crypto is in the early innings of its development, the investment landscape around it is constantly changing. One thing that plagues crypto is its sustainability issue, and fears that Bitcoin mining is bad for the environment. I am very hopeful that the crypto world will address this environmental issue, as they could scare away large institutions and even retail investors if they don't. *Green* crypto coins that are more energy efficient are rising in popularity. You are now starting to see *green* Bitcoin mining companies that use, for example, solar, hydro, nuclear, or wind power.

Statistics show that 80% of restaurants fail within their first five years. I think 99.99% of all crypto coins will fail. By the way, if this happens, it will be good for Bitcoin. I am not big on altcoins, loosely defined as any crypto other than Bitcoin. Their name comes from the fact that they're alternatives to Bitcoin and traditional fiat money. Many, including myself, don't think more *coins* even need to be issued. Why don't they just go public and issue stock? There are far too many altcoins, and I think as each day passes it gives time for other technologies to catch up. I also think many crypto companies issue far too many coins, which causes them to suffer massive dilution. Some popular crypto coins, for example, have issued billions of coins. No, that is not a misprint.

According to firm security.org, 40% of American adults now own crypto as of June 2024. The rate of crypto ownership by women has surged from 18% a year ago to 29% at the start of 2024. According to data analytics firm CivicScience, the possible driver of the recent growth in crypto investing is the increasing popularity of the investment app Robinhood, which offers many crypto coins for investors to purchase. They found the percentage of U.S. adults who use or intend to use Robinhood has risen to 23%, up from 17% in 2021. Bitcoin ETFs also likely factor in to the rise. In January 2024, the Securities and Exchange Commission approved the first set of bitcoin ETFs, which offer a potentially more accessible option for investors looking to get into crypto.

The biggest spark for Bitcoin, in my opinion, will be companies buying it for their balance sheets. The publicly traded company, MicroStrategy, now has done this, but you are starting to see more corporations buying Bitcoin. Then we could see more pension funds, financial institutions, banks, countries, etc. buying Bitcoin. When large institutions start buying Bitcoin, they're smart enough not to tell you they're buying it, so as not to move the price up. Why would they want to jack the price of Bitcoin up so they would have to pay more for it? They will let you know they bought Bitcoin well after they actually bought it. At that point, you may regret not buying Bitcoin yourself when it was much cheaper than its current price. As society becomes more educated and interested in crypto, I can only predict that there could be a lot of runway ahead, and a lot of opportunity for future gains. As always, do your own research and thinking on Bitcoin. I am only expressing my opinion on crypto and Bitcoin.

Michael Saylor, whose firm is the largest corporate holder of Bitcoin, refers to Bitcoin not as a currency, but as digital property. He calls it "Manhattan in cyberspace." I like this metaphor. Both land in Manhattan and Bitcoin are scarce and desirable, Saylor says. Land prices go up because you can't print more land. In the last 200 years, the price of real estate in Manhattan has continually gone up and gotten more valuable. Investing in Bitcoin could be like investing in land in Manhattan, and Bitcoin could have even more advantages than land in Manhattan. One could argue an advantage Bitcoin has over a piece of Manhattan real estate is that Bitcoin is portable. Another key advantage is that there is a very low barrier to entry to acquiring and owning Bitcoin. You can invest even just $10 in it if you wanted, and you can do this very quickly and easily.

Bitcoin's design ensures that ownership is indisputable, and transactions are secure, mirroring the legal protections afforded to physical property, but in a digital context. The Bitcoin protocol is *the set of rules that govern the functioning of Bitcoin.* Bitcoin also has institutional adoption now as an ETF, and investors love ETFs. I like that Bitcoin is part of a ledger system, and has a fixed supply. Scarcity and store of value for me are Bitcoin's main selling feature and the only reasons I own it. I am sure, for example, if there were 200,000 Picasso paintings that each painting would be worth much less than if there were only 200. I see Bitcoin as an 'escape hatch' to protect myself from excessive government money printing and currency debasement.

It might sound strange to say I invest in something like Bitcoin that has so many price swings and whose chart might look like a roller coaster ride. I, however, embrace this volatility because it is more widely adopted now and it's likely not going to zero. Also, in regards to its price, Bitcoin has higher lows now, which is a good thing. There are no Bitcoin board meetings either. Bitcoin is also not going to ever file for bankruptcy, unlike any private or publicly traded company. The other thing I like about Bitcoin is its price goes up and down often, but it always seems to eventually go back up. Keep in mind that MANY stocks go down but NEVER go back up. So, in a sense, Bitcoin is resilient.

Some investors are afraid to invest in Bitcoin, as they consider it high-risk. That is understandable. But let's take a look at a company that everyone knows, and many would consider a 'safe' investment: Starbucks, which even pays a dividend. I love the place. I enjoy their mocha lattes and breakfast sandwiches. Many think Bitcoin is a risky investment, in comparison. Well, let's compare the last 5 years of total returns of both (as of time of writing) and see which investment is 'riskier' and which one had the higher overall return, had you invested in either or both of them 5 years ago. The results here speak for themselves, and, apparently, if you invested in Starbucks stock you lost money.

Starbucks stock overall return *down* 12%

Bitcoin overall return *up* 483%

I only randomly picked Starbucks to compare returns to Bitcoin. I could have easily substituted many other well-known publicly traded companies. 'Strong and stable' companies Disney, PayPal, and Nike all had *negative* total stock returns the last five years as well.

There is compound interest, which many call the Eighth Wonder of the World. What most forget, though, is compound inflation, the Ninth Wonder of the World. This book is not about inflation, so I won't spend a lot of time on it, other than to mention it is currently trending higher at time of writing. The true rate of inflation is likely much higher than what is even being reported. The word for permanent inflation is called compound inflation, and I am pretty sure we have this throughout the entire world. If you are looking to buy a house now you will likely understand what I mean. What is not debatable is the U.S. Government (and other countries) printing money is a major contributing factor to inflation. Currency debasement is when a currency is debased, and therefore loses value. Sooner or later, people catch on and begin demanding higher prices for the goods they sell or more wages for their work, resulting in inflation. To myself and many other investors, Bitcoin can be a hedge against currency debasement and inflation.

When the Federal Reserve prints trillions of dollars, more money gets produced, which effectively reduces the value of each individual dollar. When you give people money, they go out and spend it. You then have too many dollars chasing too few goods. What gets inflated first, though, is the money supply. This is important to understand. Then, of course, the prices of goods and services get inflated too. The increase in the money supply eventually causes the price of everything to go up.

Bitcoin can be a hedge against currency debasement. Governments throughout the world printed and spent trillions in their pandemic related efforts beginning in 2020. The total fiscal response of the United States to Covid-19 amounted to a staggering 25% of its Gross Domestic Product (GDP.) I feel one must view the U.S. dollar as being under attack (debased) and people are looking to move their cash into other assets that can outpace currency debasement and inflation.

I view the 'duality' of Bitcoin and U.S. dollars. You never really hear anyone speak about this. Many people, it seems, view Bitcoin as mostly a store of value. They're not buying Bitcoin; They're transferring dollars to Bitcoin. I personally plan on holding most of my Bitcoin, just like I don't plan on selling my house next week either. I am willing to sit and wait for the price of Bitcoin to keep appreciating. The store of value of Bitcoin just means you hold it and think it will be worth more in the future. I do not want to spend any of my Bitcoin right now, but I do want to pay for and spend on things with my almost worthless U.S. dollars. Banks offer something called credit cards, where you can spend dollars without having to own them. So, you can spend the thing that only goes down, without actually having to own it, while hoarding the thing that only hopefully goes up (Bitcoin). In a sense, you should be shorting the U.S. dollar by the way you live your financial life. It should be mentioned that it is ok to use your credit card, as long as you try to payoff your balance every month.

I think both Bitcoin and the U.S. dollar can co-exist. I want to adopt Bitcoin to store my wealth, and dollars to spend my wealth. I view this as a two-currency system, whereas before Bitcoin we only had the U.S. dollar. Bitcoin has been one of the best performing assets over the past ten years by far, and the U.S. dollar has only been going down. Wouldn't you want to own the thing that for the most part only goes up (Bitcoin) vs something that only goes down in purchasing power (the U.S. dollar)?

In my opinion, Bitcoin has gone up so much in value because the world is so screwed up. If worldwide inflation and currency debasement didn't exist, then I'm pretty sure Bitcoin would not do well. Keep in mind, though, that these were the exact reasons Bitcoin was even created.

Regarding risk, many think Bitcoin is very high risk. Most people would likely tell you that Bitcoin is a risky investment and gold is a very safe investment. They may be right, but you should factor in the return of an asset was well, not just its risk. As I write this now it is late August of 2024. The year is almost over and Bitcoin is up about 40% year-to-date and gold is up around 22% for the year.

CHAPTER 16
RULE OF 72

I n finance, the Rule of 72 is a formula that estimates the amount of time it takes for an investment to double in value, if it is earning a fixed annual rate of return. The simple calculation is to divide the number 72 by the annual expected interest rate you hope to achieve. So, for example, at an annual interest rate of return of 10%, you would divide 72 by 10 and it would take approximately 7.2 years to double your money. At the other extreme, if your money sits in a standard savings account and earns just 0.09% (the average interest rate for savings accounts nationwide at the time I wrote my first investing book *Night Trading* in 2021), it would take you approximately **800 years** to double your money. You can see the importance of trying to earn the most amount of interest, or capital appreciation, on your hard-earned money.

I am always looking to at least double my money in any stock or investment. That is the benchmark. I imagine anyone that invests feels similarly and wants to make a great return. The faster you can get your investment to double is obviously better. What I like about this rule is it's not only simple to understand, but enables you to set a goal that answers the question: How long will it take to double my money?

The S&P 500 Index is a benchmark of stock market performance. The index has returned a historic annualized average return of around 10% (less inflation) since its inception. At the very least, I always try to earn at least that rate of return on my money. However, any good year, say a 30% return, could significantly decrease the total number of years to doubling, assuming the other years stay true to averaging at least a 10% return. I am always, therefore, on the lookout for investments that can earn more than 10% per year, if possible. This rule is the benchmark, and if I can cut down the number of years to double my money then that is obviously only a good thing. It is useful to use this Rule of 72 simply as an overall financial goal.

I like to focus on how fast I can double my money, both in my overall portfolio and individual stocks. I don't like to sell if I don't need the money, and I think the company is still a solid investment. This old Rule of 72 is still applicable in today's investment environment, because in certain types of investments you can double your money very quickly; case in point is Bitcoin and the many other cryptocurrencies, or even options trading many stocks. Some stocks have doubled in a matter of just months. By the way, take note of the word "can" in this paragraph.

CHAPTER 17
WHEN TO SELL A STOCK

When it comes to investing, the decision of when to buy a stock can often be much easier than knowing the right time to sell. Buying a stock is fairly simple, and anyone of age can buy a stock if they have the money. Even a teenager could buy a stock. So, when should you sell a stock?

This is a difficult question to answer, because there isn't a definitive or correct answer. Warren Buffett's favorite holding period is forever, as he often remarks, but it doesn't always work out that way, and it is not realistic to hold any stock forever. Even Warren Buffett sells many of his stocks, just not very often. Peter Lynch, one of the most successful stock investors ever, never used stop-losses. Lynch admitted he was never in a hurry to sell a stock. Stop-loss orders are used to limit loss on existing positions. A stop-loss order instructs that a stock be sold when it reaches a specified price, known as the stop price. If a stock is falling rapidly, this gets you out of the stock before your potential loss gets ugly. Many successful investors use stops. In contrast to Peter Lynch, famous and successful stock investor Mark Minervini often uses stop losses. The 'when to sell' question also assumes you are selling *all* of your shares, and that may not always be the case, as you can sell *some* of your shares and keep the rest.

While Buffett and Lynch like to hold onto their stocks for a long time, other successful and famous investors don't like to hold onto a stock when it drops. When you read and study the best and most successful stock investors, the common theme is to cut your losses. To come to grips with this, you must admit to yourself that you are wrong. You need to accept that your thesis is not playing out. Maybe you are 'right' on the stock, but the stock market is making a big correction to the downside. If you really love the stock, you can always sell your shares and buy back into the stock at a lower price. I tend to hold stocks longer than most, both on the way up and on the way down. I would not necessarily try to mimic myself. I try not to sell a great, quality stock I own that is going up. Conversely, when a stock I own drops, I tend to sell near the 50-day and 200-day moving averages. Moving averages are discussed in detail in Chapter 22. If I had to tally it up, I've been burned more in the stock market throughout my life by selling a great stock, rather than holding it when it dropped. In my personal experience, many of those stocks went on to go up significantly just a few years later. Conversely, around 50% of the time, a stock I sold ended up going down even farther after I sold. So, there is that to consider.

In the next section, I am going to give an example of a stock I owned a few years back that took a big hit and dropped in price. I sold it because I thought it would fall further. Well, selling that stock later proved to be one of the worst investing decisions of my life. Let's discuss….

Vistra (ticker: VST) is a leading Fortune 500 integrated retail electricity and power generation company based in Irving,

Texas. Vistra is the largest competitive power generator company in the U.S., with enough capacity to power 20 million homes. I started buying Vistra stock in late 2020, mostly because I thought it would be a safe investment, as they were a utility company and also paid a dividend. What could possibly go wrong? Well, not many months after purchasing their stock, I came across this headline while scrolling through my news feed:

April 26, 2021 (Reuters) - U.S. energy company Vistra Corp boosted the negative impact of winter storm Uri in Texas in February to about $1.6 billion from its prior estimate of $900 million to $1.3 billion. Vistra said the new estimate excludes any recovery from the potential success of its various legal and regulatory challenges related to the storm.

There was a rare cold spell and snowstorm in Texas that paralyzed the entire state. By the way, how often do you see snowstorms in Texas? Most of the state lost power due to the extremely cold weather. The Texas Department of State Health Service reported 246 people died in the storm, with close to two-thirds of the deaths due to hypothermia. The utility company had a contractual obligation to provide power to residents and unfortunately had to absorb $1.2 billion dollars in cost overruns. I didn't want to wait around many years for them to make up that huge financial hit, so I sold the stock. Luckily, I got out of my trade pretty much unscathed. I suffered a small loss, but nothing major. The worst part, though, was yet to come. This stock came back to haunt me a few years later.

Vistra stock eventually recovered, and in a big way. Using round numbers, I sold the stock at around $20, but the stock four years later was trading for over $100 per share. If I had just held onto my shares, I could have made five times my original investment, a cool 500% gain. Who would have ever thought a boring utility stock could one day trade like a high-flying technology or semiconductor stock? I certainly never thought of this when I first bought Vistra stock. But who would have ever thought a deadly ice and snow storm could shut down the entire state of Texas? By the way, the reason Vistra stock went up so much was they became a player in the AI, artificial intelligence space. They are viewed as fueling the massive boom in demand for electricity to power artificial intelligence data centers. You can see Vistra's rapid stock price appreciation on the chart here (note the X axis is the year and the Y axis its stock price in U.S. dollars):

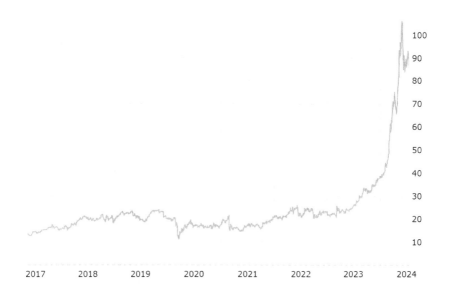

It is difficult to give one blanket answer regarding when a stock will burn out, and to sell it. Believe it or not, even the Sun will eventually burn out. Astronomers estimate that the Sun has about 7 billion to 8 billion years left before it sputters out and dies. The following is from the great investing book *Richer, Wiser, Happier*: "Many believe that everything in life is on a path to fade. If you think of evolution, 99% of species that have ever existed on Earth are extinct. And businesses are no exception."

My dividend stocks are for the long term, and I usually never want to sell those. My friend, a Wall Street banker, only buys solid companies (most paying a dividend) and invests for the long term. Actually, he hasn't sold any of his stocks in the last twenty years. The polar opposite of this is the fulltime day trader. Day traders are not the type of people that buy green bananas either, and have the patience for the bananas to ripen. I know someone that 'day traded' a stock a few decades ago. They bought a stock at a very low price back then, and sold it a short time later when the stock went up $5. A nice gain at the time. That stock was Amazon (ticker: AMZN), and they sure regret selling it! They recently calculated the shares today would be worth over a million dollars if they had just held onto them. I am sure there were many others, including myself, that overlooked Amazon decades ago.

I have a rule where I will consider selling a stock if and when it goes up 100% (aka double my initial investment). At that time, I will look to see what the future projections are for the stock price. I typically have other new, undervalued, and hot stocks on my watchlist that I want to invest in. A decision should be made if you have a new stock on your watchlist; can it increase more than the stock I currently own that has already doubled? Should I take profits and sell all my shares of this stock I currently own that has doubled? In most cases, the answer for myself is yes, and no one could honestly ever fault someone for selling a stock that doubled for you. It is worth noting that during a rising bull market, there is even more pressure to sell a stock that is a laggard. You can lose patience and become frustrated if your stock is not performing well, but when you look around you see many other stock opportunities. Conversely, you can also feel pressure to sell in a bear market, but that can also be a big mistake because the stock may eventually go up again. If there is nothing fundamentally wrong with a company, then I will usually try to hold onto their stock, even if it goes down. A stock dropping could just be a function of certain outside forces and not the investment itself. You may just have to wait for the rest of the world to catch up and realize how great an investment it is. I will typically only sell if I think there is absolutely no hope for the company. If a stock is down considerably, it could be that the sector they are in went out of favor, or something outside the control of the company is affecting their stock. I find that money typically will rotate back into that particular sector in due time.

If you buy a stock already down 80% but it eventually goes down 90%, you lose 50% of your money. That might be a brain teaser for you, but the math works, and it is a correct statement. I have often made bad choices when selling stocks, and I find it a difficult and gut-wrenching decision to make, regardless of whether I have made or lost money on the stock. The biggest problem I have seen people make is selling a stock too soon, even if they don't need the money. Usually, when I sell a stock that I own, it tends to go up right after I sell it. It's not just me. I have taken an informal poll of all my friends and family over the years, and in nearly all cases everyone that sold a stock regrets selling. Almost every stock they sold; over time the stock eventually went up. Another issue to consider is that many technology companies today are so complex that no one, not even financial experts, even know how to value a lot of these companies. So, don't feel bad if you cannot figure out what share price a stock should be trading at, because it is very difficult to figure out.

One other thing I would like to mention is the topic of not being invested in the market at all. If you sell a large amount of your stocks, you are entering the realm of not being invested in the stock market. If you are in the business of trying to make money, this can potentially be a bad place to be, as by not participating, you could miss out on the opportunity to earn money in the stock market if and when it goes up. Remember, the current market price of anything you own (stocks, real estate, crypto, etc.), might not mean much until you sell it. It is best not to be overly concerned with the daily or weekly price fluctuations of your assets, if you are truly investing for the long term.

I also factor in how much competition a company has in any possible sell decision, as well as the strength and quality of those competitors. Some companies completely dominate a certain space or industry they operate, like Google dominates web searches, or Apple cell phones. If I feel the company whose stock I own cannot become the market leader, or at least reasonably compete in its space, I will consider that in my decision making.

I hope I am never in the position to have to decide to sell a stock. However, you must face the fact that you will ultimately be put in that situation. The most important thing is to do your research and pick the right stock in the first place so you can avoid having to make the difficult decision to sell, at least for a while. Sometimes, basic instincts kick in when deciding if to sell, and there is nothing wrong with that either.

CHAPTER 18
LIVING OFF THE INTEREST

I'm sure Taylor Swift doesn't need to take any investing risks. She can just put most of her money in the bank and live off the interest alone. There are two types of investors: those looking to get rich, and those who are already rich.

You may have heard the term before, "living off the interest." As it is described – the phrase means not touching your principal investment and just living off of the interest. Some may also interpret this to mean having made it to the Winner's Circle in life, so to speak – where one does not have to worry about the daily grind of working a 9 to 5 job to cover your basic living expenses. We all kind of know what it is but, honestly, it is not something attainable for most people. When I say most people, I also lump myself in that group because I am still in my peak earning years and definitely do not have enough money at this point to retire. Nor do I want to retire right now. I have witnessed first-hand what living off the interest means as I have several wealthy stock-investing friends. God bless them because they all worked hard and took risks along the way to get to that point. I never ask them how much money they have in their portfolio but I get a sense that on good stock market days their daily unrealized gains are more than what over 90% of people in America make in an entire year. This is how much they can earn in just one day from only capital appreciation of their stocks in one trading day. And that is from doing nothing. That money is just the total of the daily gains of all their individual stocks that particular day.

After witnessing how all my wealthy friends live, it got me thinking about my own retirement. Let's face it, retirement is the goal we all are trying to attain. Retirement is usually the ultimate goal of investing, no matter what age that it ultimately happens. My plan to achieve this goal is to have about 50-75% of the stocks in my portfolio be dividend-producing. We discussed dividends back in Chapter 10. I currently have all the stocks in my brokerage account enrolled in the DRIP (Dividend Reinvestment Plan), which rolls over all the dividends back into company stock. When I retire, I plan on leaving the DRIP and receiving the cash every month for living expenses.

CHAPTER 19

STOCK BETA-THE RISKINESS OF A STOCK

"There is no such thing as a safe stock. That's like saying there is such a thing as a safe race car."

MARK MINERVINI, FAMOUS STOCK INVESTOR AND AUTHOR

S tock price variability is important to consider when assessing risk. I likely triggered some people by associating beta with risk in the title of this chapter, but I think a lot of that thinking is just semantics. Go tell someone a Bitcoin mining company with a beta of 4 is not risky. Beta can be a useful indicator of risk. Beta is a measure of a stock's volatility in relation to the overall market. It can be a useful metric to determine how a stock's price may move in relation to the overall market by examining its past performance. The overall market has a beta of 1.0, and individual stocks are ranked according to how much they deviate from the market. A stock with a beta of 1.0 will tend to move higher and lower in lockstep with the overall market. Stocks with a beta greater than 1.0 tend to be more volatile than the market, and those with betas below 1.0 tend to be less volatile than the underlying index.

Just like children's toys or certain household chemical cleaners, stocks also come with a warning label. That warning is the stock's beta, and you can find it online. This just happens to be the beta of Tesla stock, which is fairly high and quite a bit more than the standard beta of 1.0 of the S&P 500 Index. As such, many consider Tesla a volatile and risky stock, which it has been and continues to be. The graphic here is from the Yahoo Finance website.

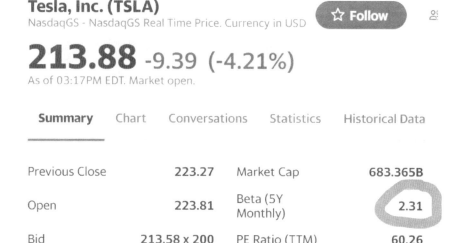

Keep in mind, a high beta doesn't necessarily imply that a stock is risky or volatile, and a low beta doesn't necessarily imply that a stock is safe. The point is that beta is just one piece of the puzzle, and is useful for predicting overall volatility and price movements. Does a high beta mean a stock is riskier? High-beta stocks are typically riskier, but they have the potential for higher returns. If a stock deviates less than the market does, the stock will have a beta below 1.0. Low-beta stocks have less risk, but they also generally provide lower returns. This last sentence is too logical, though, and remember the stock market is not always logical. Often, the stock market does the opposite of what investors think is normal. We'll talk about low-beta stock outperformance later in this chapter, as well as in even greater detail in the next chapter.

How to Calculate Beta for Your Portfolio

The key is to know the beta of your portfolio, and calculating it is quite simple. Let's presume you own five low-beta stocks, which account for 90% of your portfolio, with the remainder of your portfolio in the high-beta stock Coinbase (ticker: COIN), which has a very high beta of 3.40.

Multiply each stock's beta by its percentage of your portfolio, and then add the figures. You can see in the chart how just one high beta stock can greatly increase the overall beta/volatility of your entire portfolio. That high beta stock is only 10% of your portfolio but shockingly nearly doubles overall portfolio beta.

A Sample Portfolio's Beta

Stock	Beta	% of Portfolio	Beta Weighting
Hershey Foods	0.35	18%	0.06
PepsiCo	0.53	18%	0.10
Procter & Gamble	0.40	18%	0.07
Dollar General	0.43	18%	0.08
Duke Energy	0.44	18%	0.08
Coinbase	3.40	10%	0.34
PORTFOLIO BETA			**0.73**

Tip: You can get the beta from some of the sites discussed in Chapter 2: <u>Free Investing Information</u>. I also crosscheck beta to the beta on TipRanks website, just for additional accuracy.

I own approximately fifteen stocks, and I calculated my portfolio beta to be 1.37. I have a couple high beta stocks which skewed my data but I am generally satisfied with this beta. If anything, I feel it's a bit high, so I may try to trim my beta down a little bit to a less volatile number, likely in the 1.20 range. To do that, I will probably sell a few of my risky high beta investments and put that money into some lower beta stocks.

Please calculate your portfolio's beta. Is it close to 1? Is it within your tolerance for risk? Remember that a stock's beta will change over time, because it compares the stock's return with the returns of the overall market. Beta is merely an observation about a stock's return over a sample period, and not a permanent, immutable characteristic of that stock. It is very easy to just go to a free financial website to quickly find your stock's beta. I do this myself about once or twice a year.

Since this is a chapter discussing risk, I figured it would be appropriate to find out what someone who I admire, and have a lot of respect for, thinks about stock investing and risk. Barbara Corcoran is a businesswoman and television personality, appearing on the widely popular show *Shark Tank* for many years. Corcoran's expertise, and how she became extremely wealthy, was real estate. She founded The Corcoran Group, a real estate brokerage in New York City, which she later sold for $66 million. Corcoran's advice to succeed in life is to find something you're good at and focus mostly on that. For her, she wasn't good at stock investing, but she was very good at real estate. She said she "put all her eggs in one basket" because she really knows that basket. I can relate to her advice, because I know a few people, and have some close friends, that are not very good at stock investing. In fact, they are very bad at it. This is not a knock on them, and some of my friends will readily admit they are bad at stock investing. They could read twenty books on stock investing, maybe even my book, and still not be good at it. In that case, investing only in index funds, gold, or even cash, might not be a bad idea for them. Remember, many say that not losing your money is the first goal of investing. I concur. If you recall, I gave many examples of people losing money in the stock market in the Introduction of my book here. Corcoran talks about how when she sold her real estate business for $66 million, she put all that money in her checking account, earning almost zero interest for four years. She knew how to make money in her real estate business, but she admits she had no idea how to invest her money and make money on that money.

To wrap up, one of the key questions this chapter sought to answer is: Can low-beta stocks still provide great returns? Indeed, they can, and a paper from Harvard Business School published in September of 2013 (*The Low Beta Anomaly: A Decomposition into Micro and Macro Effects*) suggested that low beta stocks outperform the broader market over time. That thought, and this entire chapter, are a perfect handoff to the next chapter on Hershey Foods, which we will find out is a low-beta stock that greatly outperformed the S&P 500 Index over a long time period.

CHAPTER 20
HERSHEY FOODS VS THE S&P 500

I have a friend that lives in Hershey, Pennsylvania. I have been out there many times over the years to visit him. Over the last 25 years, he has been a Hershey Foods (ticker: HSY) stockholder, accumulating many shares over that time period. I chose this particular stock to analyze because it is one that most everyone in the world can relate to. I would venture a guess that most people have at some point in their life consumed a Hershey Foods product. I know I have. Hershey Foods has recently expanded heavily into snacks, with their Skinny Pop popcorn and Dot's Pretzels leading the way.

I wanted to see how this iconic and financially successful company stacked up against the S&P 500 Index over the last decade. I wondered: What if you just landed here from Mars, had zero investment knowledge, and no time to do any stock research? What would your investment return have been if you had just put all your money into a stock with even less volatility, or possibly risk, than the S&P 500 Index? This stock is Hershey Foods.

Know that, with a beta of 1.0, the S&P 500 is not without risk. If the S&P 500 has a beta of 1.0 and Hershey Foods has a beta of .35, one could conclude based on beta that Hershey Foods is likely a less volatile, or risky, investment than the S&P 500. Note: Stock beta was explained in the last Chapter 19, where an entire chapter was devoted to beta. It is apparent from the data you are about to read next that Hershey Foods beat the S&P 500.

One knock on Hershey Foods is that it is not a 'cheap' stock to buy, meaning it never really goes on sale. You will likely be paying a premium for Hershey whenever you decide to buy it. Don't get sticker shock when you see the share price or the P/E ratio of Hershey- approximately $194 and 19.0 at time of writing. However, even if you compare Hershey to another market leader in the consumer goods sector, PepsiCo, you will find very similar numbers at a $170 per share stock price and 25.0 P/E ratio. This is just the price you pay for a low beta, solid company, with a good and reliable dividend. I also think Hershey Foods has a lot of intellectual property built into its share price; for example, there is no close approximation for a Kit Kat or Reese's Peanut Butter Cup.

From 2010 to 2020, the Dow Jones Industrial Average generated a 12.6% average annual return (including dividends). The Dow Jones Industrial Average, Dow Jones, or simply the Dow, is a stock market index of thirty prominent companies listed on stock exchanges in the United States. The S&P 500 did even better, returning 13.75%. Hershey returned 14.42%, and this return does not even include their dividend. Hershey Foods paid a healthy and consistent dividend over that time. Hershey Foods is the winner over the S&P 500 over that ten-year span, albeit not by much. It appears that Hershey Foods is a recession-proof and apparently pandemic-proof business. The irony is that you need little to no investment knowledge to beat the S&P 500 in this particular case. Speaking in terms of stock beta, you would have done so with much less volatility and risk than investing in the S&P 500 Index itself.

So, what did this prove? I think it proved two very important and interesting things. First, a low beta stock still can provide great returns (comprised of both capital appreciation and dividends.) Second, that low beta stock Hershey Foods can actually outperform the S&P 500 over that ten-year period. Those are some *sweet* returns!

Let us zoom out over a much longer timeframe to see how Hershey Foods stock performed against the S&P 500. Keep in mind, Hershey Food stock started having its worst drawdown ever, starting in 2023, and continuing in 2024. Let us examine how this huge $100 per share drawdown affected Hershey stock's overall return. The time periods below are **from January, 2000 thru July 2024** and with all dividends reinvested.

Hershey Foods (ticker: HSY) **up 1,264%** with a beta of .35

S&P 500 **up 528%** with a beta of 1.0

(source: the return calculator on ofdollar-sanddata website)

Keep in mind, Hershey stock was obliterated for two years of this study, as their stock dropped approximately $100. Yet, Hershey stock *still* managed to demolish the returns of the S&P 500. Speaking of getting demolished, the S&P 500 was flat from 2000-2011, as its total return was almost zero. From 2000-2011, the S&P 500 was up a paltry 0.5% per year. After accounting for inflation, you would have lost 2% per year, making for a lost decade and then some. Meanwhile, during that eleven-year 'dry' span from 2000-2011, Hershey Foods stock returned about 250%. This is quite stunning, and further solidifies the idea that you should diversify your stock portfolio.

Let's say you wanted to look for another low beta, low risk stock to see how it compares to the S&P 500. Let's use a stock I own: Brown & Brown Insurance Brokers (ticker: BRO). I picked this stock to use in my analysis here not only because I own it, but also that I prior worked in the insurance brokerage industry for several years. An insurance broker acts as an intermediary between you and an insurer, all while collecting a commission. Insurance brokers might have the best business model of most any business, because have you ever heard of a business that didn't need or pay their insurance. At .82, Brown & Brown has a much higher beta than Hershey Foods, but much lower than the S&P 500 beta of 1.0. We will compare the exact same time period we just did for Hershey

Foods. So, **from January 2000 through July 2024** and with all dividends reinvested:

Brown & Brown (ticker: BRO) **up 4,816%** with a beta of .82

This chapter clearly showed Brown & Brown stock not only obliterated the S&P 500 returns, but completely destroyed Hershey Foods' stock returns of 1,264%. This chapter proves that what many people perceive as very low risk stocks can, in fact, greatly outperform.

CHAPTER 21
EASY ON THE MACRO

Macroeconomics, otherwise mostly referred to in its shortened name as simply just *macro*, is the part of economics concerned with large-scale or general economic factors, such as interest rates and national productivity of goods and services. A couple of years ago I was at a large investor conference and had a moment where I spoke face to face for seven or eight minutes with one of the supposed top economists in the country, who sometimes even appears on popular financial network shows. I came away from our conversation thinking to myself; "This person doesn't know any more about economics and macroeconomics than you or I do." Nor could they predict with any degree of certainty how stock investors and stockholders will react to news and economic events or shocks. Some would call them e*clownomists*. I have nothing personally against economists and macroeconomists, but I've tweeted before my 'easy on the macro' catchphrase when stock investing. I like some macro but it is only about 2% of my overall investing thesis. People with similar mindsets were pretty much proven correct in 2023, when, amidst some of the fastest and steepest interest rate rises in U.S. history, the stock market went up dramatically for the year despite all the negativity and despite nearly every macroeconomist and economist predicting gloom and doom for everyone. Most of these macroeconomists and economists had predicted huge losses in the stock markets, as well. The exact of opposite of what they said ended up happening.

I am a believer that there is always a bull/bear market going on within the overall stock market at the same time. I am not making light of any of the two following tragic historical events that happened. I am simply reporting how the stock market reacted to them.

When it comes to stock market shocks, the assassination of President John F. Kennedy on Nov. 22, 1963, ranks high in Wall Street history. The stock market is typically resilient to geo-political events, especially once Wall Street determines that the economy will not be irreparably harmed by the event. In fact, after the JFK assassination, the market regained all its losses two days later.

If you want to study longer periods of unrest, then think back to the Great Depression in the 1930s, where not every stock went down. Believe it or not, in the 1930s, there were stocks in the food, industrials and manufacturing sectors that still did well. Entertainment and movie companies did well too. I'd imagine if we had a prolonged economic downturn now that entertainment stocks like Netflix would go up. Netflix stock did, in fact, go up a lot during and after the Covid-19 pandemic in 2020. After all, what else are you going to do to entertain yourself during a pandemic.

The stock market tends to be resilient, and many investors take advantage of depressed prices and 'buy the dip.' Both

Boeing and Chrysler made more money during the Great Depression than they did before it. Chrysler went from a 9% market share in 1929 to a 24% market share in 1933. Proctor and Gamble also increased their sales during the Depression. A brand-new thing called grocery stores became popular, and better selection and lower prices kept them in business. From the Great Depression in the 1930s, and up to around 1954, there were still many stocks that went up. It's obvious, though, that only an extremely small percentage of people had money during that time period to invest in stocks.

So, to sum up, I personally feel most macroeconomics information is useless in regards to me being a successful stock investor. The bottom line for me and all that really matters is the stock price, and how the stock reacts to the macro or economic environment. The consumer price index, commonly abbreviated and known as CPI, is a price index, the price of a weighted average basket of consumer goods and services purchased by households. The producer price index, or PPI, is a monthly estimate of the weighted average prices U.S. producers (suppliers, wholesalers, etc.) receive for the products and services they create, mostly for other businesses. But, I am not trading or investing in the unemployment rate, or the CPI, or the PPI. I am trading the stock, and I mostly care just about the stock price.

CHAPTER 22

TECHNICAL ANALYSIS: YOU DON'T NEED TO CIRCUMCISE A MOSQUITO

"The value of technical analysis in the stock market is to reduce risk."

-FROM THE BOOK *THE NATURE OF RISK*

Technical stock analysis is the study of historical market data, including price and volume, to predict future price movements. As the title of this chapter so eloquently implies, we don't need to get too technical and drive ourselves crazy overanalyzing and overthinking stock charts to achieve success. This chapter is entirely about stock charts, and how we can learn to use them to hopefully make some money. With technical analysis you mostly need a compass, not necessarily a GPS, to help you find the optimal price to buy or sell a stock.

Technical analysis, as you will soon see, is mostly using data in charts to help make decisions. Keep in mind, though, that every decision can lead to failure. This is just how life works. Technical analysis (hereafter, referred to simply as "TA") is important. However, there are many other tools in the toolbox besides staring at squiggly lines on your computer screen.

As I stated earlier in this book, TA makes up about 15% of my overall investing thesis. I mostly use it to see how low I think a stock could go. Technically, the highest a stock can go is infinity, and the lowest it can go is zero. I mostly use TA to look for possible entry points. It may sound elementary, but the advice I give people is that "you want to be in the stocks that are going up." Sounds kindergarten-ish and simple, but it's true. There is always both a bull and bear market going on within the stock market at the same time. Even in the severe bear market of 2022, many stocks still went up.

Top investors will tell you to invest in and own the true market leaders; stocks charts that are 'up and to the right' and making new 52-week highs. However, a stock can't make a new 52-week high unless 1.) its stock chart is 'up and to the right,' and 2.) it has previously made a 52-week high.

There is a former Wall Street and current options trader on Financial Twitter who speaks critically about using TA. He claims in a video on his website that TA is useless and cannot accurately predict anything regarding stock prices. Keep in mind, though, that he worked on Wall Street for several decades and then went into business himself starting a large stock trading group. He now mostly uses the news and sentiment to trade stocks. He has a live trading room, and publicly posts almost all his trades on Financial Twitter. From the looks of it, he appears to be highly successful. This trader found what method to invest works for him, and that is fine. There is no 'right' way to invest. Just find the method that works best for you.

Stock charts only tell you what happened. This makes logical sense, because, technically, everything in life is in the past. Some of my largest winners, like Celsius Energy drink (ticker: CELH), Texas Roadhouse (ticker: TXRH), and Investors Savings Bank (eventually bought out by Citizens Financial Group -ticker: CFG) I must confess I barely ever looked at their stock charts the entire time I owned those stocks. If you recall, I spent all of Chapter 4 discussing my investment in Citizens Bank in detail.

I use TA as a risk management tool, not a predictive tool. Some of TA may be predictive, but probably only a small percentage, since no one can accurately predict the future. The way I personally approach stock investing is to try not to be predictive, and instead simply make a probabilistic assessment of what is likely to happen with a stock. You make your money in the buying. In the widely popular book *Rich Dad Poor Dad*, author Robert Kiyosaki said that "profit is made when you buy, not when you sell."

In the charts throughout the rest of this chapter, you will see tiny vertical bars. These are called "candlesticks," and it is important to understand them. They provide a visual representation of price movements, summarizing important information a trader or investor needs to know in one single vertical bar. You might also hear candlesticks being referred to as "Japanese candlesticks," because they were first used in Japan in the 18th century. They are widely used because they show so much information in a very simple format. Candlestick charts can be set to show different time periods, depending on what timeframe you find most useful. They are available with durations from one minute, meaning a new candle will form every minute, up to one month. Personally, I use a mix of daily, weekly, and monthly timeframes. You can set candlestick charts to the time period you want, depending on the type of trading you are undertaking. It's often advisable to look at longer time periods first, giving you an idea of the overall trend and key support and resistance levels for the stock. The support level is where the stock price regularly stops falling and bounces back up, while the resistance level is where the price normally stops rising and dips back down.

You might not realize it, or even think about it, but when you buy a stock, you are also buying its stock chart. One of the best tips I have gotten on stock investing and chart analysis comes from Anmol Singh, also known as Delta Ninety on his social media platforms, a professional full-time trader from Manhattan: Trade and invest in stocks with "low downside risk", Singh preaches. He has said this a few times on podcast interviews that he has appeared. Singh would say "the bigger the top, the bigger the drop." You might have to rewire your brain to not always think about the stocks that have the highest upside, but also ones that have low downside risk.

Many seasoned investors say you can't control the upside of a stock, but you can control the downside, which means selling a stock that is rapidly falling to avoid a big potential loss. If you take a look at the stock chart of a high-flying tech stock with a steep 'V' shaped pattern, well that stock also has a higher chance of falling. In simple terms, a stock that just rose dramatically has a higher chance of falling dramatically. To me, a 'stair step' pattern on a stock chart is better than a short, fast steep rise.

Singh talks about 'mean reversion,' how most stocks eventually revert to their mean. In the case of stock investing, this is often their 50-day and 200-day moving averages. Moving averages are discussed in detail later in this chapter. Mean reversion is something even comedian Jerry Seinfeld refers to in an old episode of his *Seinfeld* comedy show called "Even Steven." In this episode, Jerry realizes that he "breaks even" on just about everything that happens in his life. Seinfeld would say you lose a twenty-dollar bill you might then find a twenty-dollar bill. Your girlfriend breaks up with you just find another girlfriend. You lose your job then you get another job. Seinfeld says everything in life eventually reverts to the mean. Seinfeld is right.

Price Consolidation And Establishing A Base

Have you ever been to a supermarket? Obviously, yes. You like to go there because, at a single place, you can buy all the food or other items you need. The stock market works the same way. It is a supermarket where shares of a company are bought and sold. However, there is one catch. The prices of products in a supermarket are fixed, but in the stock market, the prices of stocks vary every second because of supply and demand. This process to see which direction the price of the stock heads can take many days, weeks, months, or even years to play out. And for the stock price to go up a lot, you typically need some sort of positive catalyst.

The way I learned stock charting, and the simplest method of using charting, in my opinion, is to look for stocks that are basing or consolidating. The term basing refers to the consolidation in the price of a stock, when a stock's price moves within a relatively small range. You will see later in this chapter how this visually looks in a stock chart. It will appear flat, or sideways, as the price of the stock shows that supply and demand are relatively equal. Look for a simple pattern with a big, wide base in a stock chart to try to tell the likelihood the stock may eventually break out and go higher. There is an old, and very useful, saying in the stock investing world: "The bigger the base, the higher the stock can go into space."

There are a few reasons why looking for stocks with bases that have formed over the course of weeks, months, or even many years is advantageous. First, large bases take time to form because they are caused by steady accumulation, typically by larger institutions. This means there is steady and consistent long-term demand for the stock. Second, if stocks with these bases break out to the upside, it is a sign that buyers are in control of the stock's long-term trend. An excellent visual representation is to look at the next chart called: Sprouts Farmers Market – Chart 1 on the upcoming page. It is very easy to witness the 'basing' taking place over several years. You can clearly see the stock trading 'sideways' for many years, before eventually turning sharply higher.

Cup-With-Handle

You can think of a cup-with-handle stock chart pattern as a U-shaped base with handle. Many stocks can base, or consolidate, for years, even decades.

Sprouts Farmers Market (ticker: SFM) went public in 2013. I own this stock and it is one of my favorite stocks in my portfolio. I also shop there. Their chart here shows the 'cup' or 'U-shaped' base. As you can see in their chart below, their 'cup' has been forming for about a decade. The 'cup' is so big you could practically sit in it and take a nice bubble bath. One could also call this a 'cup with no handle,' though, because the 'handle' has not even formed yet.

To me, Sprouts is a fascinating stock and stock chart to examine. You would think, and may have been taught, that you always need large institutions buying for a stock to go up dramatically. However, in the Sprouts chart below, you can see how fiercely the stock rose in the past several years, while the share volume bars on the very bottom are in a descending trend. This trend is shown by the downward sloping arrow. The reason could be that large institutions might not want to leave big footprints (massive daily purchases of a stock) of stocks they want to accumulate, as they don't want to move the price up too fast as they accumulate their own large position. Institutional accumulation may not always be so obvious.

A more obvious example of large institutional stock accumulation would be Zoom (ticker: ZM) stock accumulation when the Covid pandemic hit in March 2020. If you pulled up the Zoom stock chart from back then, you can clearly see massive, and fast, institutional accumulation. If you would like to see an exact number of institutions that currently hold any stock that you own, you can easily find this on the Yahoo Finance website. Put in your stock ticker at the top and then go to the *Holders* section.

Sprouts Farmers Market: Chart 1 (from Finviz)

The Sprouts stock chart cup-with-handle pattern has not played out yet. This is due to the fact that Sprouts stock has gone up so fast that it never formed the handle. This is good for investors like me that own Sprouts stock and love to see the price go up rapidly, but bad to show you a full cup-with-handle pattern. To get a better example of the cup-with-handle pattern, we'll look at a very popular stock that I own and probably most people have at least heard of: Google (ticker: GOOG)

As you can see below in a weekly timeframe for Google, I have marked the 'cup' and the 'handle.' The arrow points up and to the right, as Google's stock price heads up. The cup-with-handle is one of the most popular, widely recognized, and potentially bullish stock patterns out there. A good way to remember the cup-with-handle stock pattern is to just think of the glass or ceramic cup that holds your coffee or tea. It looks like that, more or less. You may notice that the bottom of the cup in the Google chart below is a bit 'jagged' and not totally smooth, but it's close enough. Remember, I prior said that TA is not perfect.

Note: Google chart here from Finviz

Moving Averages, Support, And Resistance

A moving average is an indicator that investors use to determine the direction of a trend. It is called a "moving" average because it is continually recalculated based on the latest price data. A stock's moving average represents its average price over a set time period.

There are some different moving averages, but for the purposes of this book we'll use the simple moving average. Common moving average lengths are 10, 20, 50, 100, and 200 days. When I visited the New York Stock Exchange last year, I met people there that look at 200-week moving averages, and even longer back than that. For most investors, though, you really don't need to look that far back. Because it relies on looking backward at stock pricing, the moving average is a lagging indicator. It is generally used to confirm how a stock's price has been trending, though it doesn't necessarily guarantee that a particular trend will continue. In my opinion, the best and easiest place to get the 50 and 200-day moving averages is the Yahoo Finance website. Can just click on the Statistics button to take you there. A 50-day moving average is equal to the average price that all investors paid for the asset over the past 10 trading weeks (or two and a half months), making it a commonly used support level. Similarly, the 200-day moving average represents the average price over the past 40 trading weeks.

What can you use the moving average for? If a stock's price approaches its moving average, some use that price as a reference point to either buy or sell the stock. When a stock falls below its moving average, it means that investors may be losing confidence in the stock, and some may consider selling their shares if the price continues to decrease. Someone might sell their stock if it breaks below its 50 or 200-day moving average. On the other hand, if the stock breaks above the 50 or 200-day moving average, it indicates a bullish trend. This means that the trend may be moving up as investors have more confidence in the stock and consider buying.

"Boring" Accounting And The 50% Profit *Shopify* Swing Trade

In this section I will teach you how I made a 50% return in just four months, in hopes that maybe you can do this yourself someday. This was a trade, so I got in and then got completely out of the stock in four months.

Many investors have fantastical ways of analyzing stocks, but what about good old boring accounting, which is what a company ultimately comes down to. The company either makes money or it doesn't make money. You rarely see stock 'experts' talk about the financials of a company, likely because most do not understand accounting, which in and of itself is somewhat complicated. You don't need to be a CPA, but the more you know about accounting can't hurt. Warren Buffett has said there's nothing more important to understand than accounting: "People ask me what they should take in business school," Buffett said. "You have to understand accounting. It's the language. It's like being in a foreign country without knowing the language if you're in business and you don't understand accounting." In the graphic below, I will go over a live trade that I did using accounting, combined with TA to score a nice 50% gain in only four months. The stock 'swing trade' discussed is Shopify (ticker: SHOP). Shopify is a Canadian multinational ecommerce company. Shopify is the name of its proprietary e-commerce platform for online stores and retail point-of-sale systems.

If Warren Buffett says we need to understand accounting, then here goes. The Financial Accounting Services Board's rules for impairment charges of goodwill outline that companies must determine the fair market value of assets on a regular basis. The goodwill impairment test involves comparing the asset to its fair market value to see if the fair market value has declined below the reported value. If so, impairment must be done. Impairment charge is a term used to account for an asset that is no longer as valuable as it may have once been. It usually occurs during unforeseen events that negatively affect a company.

This Shopify trade was based on the impairment charge I highlighted in the graphic of their financials below. An impairment charge is a process used by businesses *to write off worthless goodwill or report a reduction in the value of* goodwill. As you can see in the graphic below, Shopify took a $1.3 billion one-time impairment charge in Q2 on the sale of their logistics business. It was easy to tell that when Shopify reported for Q3, and this charge was no longer there then obviously their financials would look far better. Their report even said this, and I quote: "Excluding these one-time charges, operating income was positive for the quarter."

Shopify Inc.
Condensed Consolidated Statements of Operations and Comprehensive Loss
(Expressed in US millions, except share and per share amounts, unaudited)

	Three months ended		Six months ended	
	June 30, 2023	June 30, 2022	June 30, 2023	June 30, 2022
	$	$	$	$
Revenues				
Subscription solutions	444	366	826	711
Merchant solutions	1,250	929	2,376	1,788
	1,694	1,295	3,202	2,499
Cost of revenues				
Subscription solutions	85	85	169	163
Merchant solutions	774	554	1,481	1,042
	859	639	1,650	1,205
Gross profit	835	656	1,552	1,294
Operating expenses				
Sales and marketing	321	327	608	630
Research and development	648	347	1,106	651
General and administrative	131	130	254	239
Transaction and loan losses	31	42	73	62
Impairment on sales of Shopify's logistics businesses	1,340	—	1,340	—
Total operating expenses	2,471	846	3,381	1,582

So, I bought Shopify stock for a swing trade in October 2023, right before they reported their Q3 earnings. You can see almost exactly where I entered the trade in <u>Shopify: Chart 1</u>. It is right where I circled and wrote 'Tight' and have an arrow pointing. Sure enough, when Shopify reported their Q3 earnings on November 2, 2023, they reported great earnings, and the stock reacted positively soon thereafter.

This Shopify trade I executed is a perfect example of both fundamental and technical analysis coming together for a highly successful trade. I entered the trade in early October 2023 at around $50/share and exited in late January 2024 at around $80/share, for around a 50% gain in about four months. The sell can clearly be seen in <u>Shopify: Chart 1</u>. You can also clearly see the stock 'gapped up' at its November 2nd, 2023 earnings. When a stock 'gaps up' it means its price went higher, which signals bullish sentiment and strong buying interest in the stock. This 'gap up' can be seen on <u>Shopify: Chart 1</u> almost exactly lined up with the second 'T' in the word tight.

Shopify: Chart 1 (from Finviz)

Shopify: Chart 2 (from Finviz)

An obvious question you might ask from looking at <u>Shopify Chart 2</u> is: Why is the stock price going up if volume is almost simultaneously thinning out? Note that I am talking about the action starting at and to the right of the beginning of the thick and thin arrows. Shopify's stock price essentially doubled in the timeframe from October 2022 to October 2023, from $28 to $58. The stock price likely went up because of the exchange of shares from weak hands to strong hands. Most of the people interacting with Shopify stock during its big runup were buyers, as most of the sellers had left. You want the stock, and its candlesticks shown here, to "tighten up." Ideally, you want to see multiple tight candlesticks and low (or lower) relative volume. Note the vertical bars at the bottom of the chart (underneath the downward sloping thin arrow) are volume bars, which graphically show the daily, weekly, or monthly volume of shares traded. This is typically expressed in millions of shares for larger volume stocks, but the unit of measure can fluctuate. You want to see all the sellers give up and sell the stock, with the only people left hopefully are only buyers of the stock. The 'tightening' indicates accumulation by buyers. The 'tight' close pattern is a TA stock pattern that occurs when a stock closes at nearly the same price for several consecutive weeks. It indicates that there is a period of indecision in the market, with buyers and sellers fairly evenly matched. This pattern is often associated with stocks that have strong fundamentals and a solid business model. The pattern was first discovered by Investor's Business Daily founder William "Bill" O'Neill.

I hope this Shopify trade example was useful to you. It is a good example to use because impairment charges are very common. These charges are easy to spot too, but you must seek them out in the company's financial statements. Impairment charges can often have a significant impact on a company's financial statements. The good news about impairment charges from a stock investor's standpoint is that these charges are typically a one-time charge, so a business can usually recover quickly from it.

Double Top and Double Bottom

Spotting reversal patterns in stock charts is key to knowing when to buy or sell a stock. The double top and double bottom patterns below illustrate this. Just remember, a double top is bad. You typically do not want to buy a stock with a pattern that looks like the McDonald's 'M'.

DOUBLE TOP = BAD

DOUBLE BOTTOM = GOOD

I love getting into trades off of a double bottom pattern. A double bottom is simply the opposite move in price as the double top pattern. The pattern indicates that, after two lows, there could be a significant increase in price. Consequently, the double bottom chart pattern resembles the letter "W." This "W" pattern forms when prices register two distinct lows on a chart. However, the definition of a true double bottom is achieved only when prices rise above the highest point of the entire formation, leaving the entire pattern behind. A double bottom chart pattern is significant because, if accurately identified, it can signal an excellent entry opportunity for investors. It indicates that the stock has reached a crucial support level, and is encountering difficulty moving lower. That implies that the stock has formed a low and is now positioned for an upward move.

You can use it to your advantage to possibly buy a quality stock off of a double bottom, when everyone else is fearful and selling the stock. One mental approach I use in investing is: If a quality stock or company like Apple or Tesla, for example, sells off dramatically you have a whole new group of buyers coming in that are going to go long the stock. So, I find it can be beneficial to buy the stalwarts, like Apple stock for example, when they have large corrections.

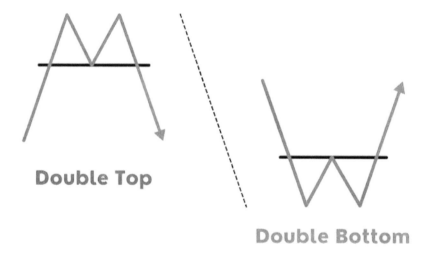

Double Top

Double Bottom

Head and Shoulders

No, head and shoulders in stock charting is not a dandruff shampoo. However, we can use dandruff as a metaphor to understand this pattern. A head and shoulders chart formation usually indicates a reversal to the downside. The neckline, as depicted in the next graphic, is the horizontal line that connects the first two troughs to one another. While no chart pattern is an accurate predictor 100% of the time, the head and shoulders pattern has historically known to be fairly reliable. It is also one of the most easily recognizable chart patterns. The chart below from The Corporate Financial Institute does a great job of showing the head and shoulders chart pattern.

Inverse Head and Shoulders

The inverse head and shoulders chart pattern is a bullish chart formation that signals a potential reversal of a downtrend. It is the opposite of the head and shoulders chart pattern, which is a bearish formation.

A good example of this is the Bitcoin chart, below.

Trendlines

It is also helpful to look at trendlines and trends. There is an old saying: "The trend is your friend." Stock charts cannot predict the future, but they can show you the trend in a stock.

Below is the stock of insurance broker Brown & Brown (ticker: BRO). As you can clearly see, the stock is trending upwards for the past seven months or so in this chart. The stock has been trading in a very defined 'channel' within that upwards trendline. This is the daily timeframe, and if you zoom out and look at the monthly timeframe over the past ten years, the stock has also performed extremely well in that timeframe too. (Note: chart below from Finviz)

Speaking of trend, I also like to follow the trend of 'seasonality' in stock investing. "Sell in May and go away" is an old market adage, popularized by the *Stock Trader's Almanac*, which reveals the best six months of the year for stocks (they used the Dow Index) occurs from November through April. It suggests investors should sell in May and wait until November to buy back into the markets. It has been proven that the six months from May through October have lower returns than the months November through April. However, the May through October period total stock returns have generally been positive. I hope no one would take the adage literally, and sell all their stocks in May. The adage just means that the stock market slows in the summer months as volume slows. The weather is nice and warm from May thru October, so you should be outside enjoying life instead of sitting home all day staring at stocks on your computer screen. You likely will also find better bargains May through October, which is kind of my takeaway from all this 'seasonality' talk.

We have just gone over a lot of TA, but really have only scratched the surface. Entire books have been written on TA. Personally, I only use what I've gone over in this chapter. You might feel differently, and that's fine. Everyone is entitled to their opinion on stock investing. Remember, there is no 'right' way to invest. There are many books out there on TA. There is a hugely popular TA book I recently read written by a professional full-time stock trader. Strangely enough, the author spent most of his own book on TA saying he uses stock charts, but does not believe they are responsible for him being a profitable trader. Keep in mind, it's been documented the guy made millions trading stocks from using TA. He discusses how TA and charting is useful, but emphasizes that your mental approach is far more important. As the title of this chapter states, you don't need to overthink or overanalyze stock charts to be a successful stock investor.

CHAPTER 23
NEIL LEIFER: THE EPITOME OF LUCK AND TIMING

L uck and timing are important components of stock investing, as well as life. I think most people don't sit back and realize, or just don't want to acknowledge, how much timing, and a little bit of luck matters to success in many things in life. You could apply this to stock investing, relationships, etc.

When you walk into my house, this Muhammad Ali boxing photo is one of the first things you see. Muhammad Ali encompassed so much and most know his story and contributions to society, but the part of the picture that relates to stock investing, and quite frankly life, is the story behind the photographer of this famous sports photo.

Many consider this picture one of the greatest sports photographs in history. The picture was taken on May 25, 1965 in Lewiston, Maine at a boxing rematch between Muhammad Ali and Sonny Liston. That day, there were two sports photographers there from *Sports Illustrated* magazine. Neil Leifer was a twenty-two-year-old sports photographer for them. Leifer was one of only two photographers with color film in his camera that day in 1965. His other coworker was fifty-three-year-old Herbert "Herb" Scharfman, an American sports photographer notable for several famous photographs of American sports people published by *Sports Illustrated* and other publications.

Herb Scharfman, the senior photographer at *Sports Illustrated,* had the first pick of seats that day, not Leifer, who was the new young kid. Scharfman is best known for appearing in Ali's famous sports photo - Neil Leifer's shot of Muhammad Ali standing over a fallen Sonny Liston. Scharfman was directly across the ring from Leifer, appearing between the legs of Ali in the iconic image. Leifer later said, "Herbie Scharfman was one of the greats, but on that night, he was in the wrong seat."

Leifer got lucky that day. If Leifer hadn't chosen the opposite side as Scharfman, he would've been stuck shooting toward Ali's back at the big moment. But when Liston fell, he fell in front of Leifer, not Scharfman. Leifer got famous for this photo and Scharfman got famous too, as the guy between Ali's leg in the picture. The questions to ask and ponder are did Neal Leifer get lucky that day when he pressed the button on his camera to take this photo? Was luck the only reason he became famous for taking this iconic picture? One would say he was lucky, but he also had the sense, skill, and experience to use color film that day. In fact, one of the main reasons that made this picture so famous was that Leifer used color film, whereas most everyone else at that time used black and white film. This also presented another problem for Leifer, because he had to do a lot more work setting up strobe lights, and they took a long time to recharge. Decades later Leifer said something about luck that will really make you think:

> *"I've always believed that you can't be in the right place at the right time unless you're in the right place all the time."*

Most everyone has probably heard the phrase about "being in the right place at the right time." This should apply to stocks too. In my opinion, stock investing is all about timing. Many other things in life are arguably so as well. What if your current wife or husband wasn't at that same bar you met at thirty years ago? What if you were born in 1890 in the United States, and during the Roaring 1920s was when you were piling lots of money into the stock market and then the 1929 Depression hit? It literally took twenty-five more years after that 1929 crash for the stock market to get back to its 1929 peak? I could go on but you get the point.

Someone from my old high school recently won about $275,000,000 in the Mega Millions lottery. This person had been spending about $20 per week on the lottery for many years. So, was it luck when they finally won? Yes, of course, but luck may not have been the entire reason they won the lottery. You could also argue they had been preparing for this moment for years. I would think if this huge lottery winner hadn't consistently been playing the lottery every single week, they would have likely not have been in that convenience store to win "the big one." This lottery winner now lives back in our hometown only a few miles from our old high school. Funny how life ends up and for him circled back to where it all started. I recently visited the convenience store where he won "the big one." I bought $20 worth of lottery tickets when the Powerball was $1 billion. As you can probably figure out, I did not win.

Warren Buffett said at his 2024 Berkshire Hathaway annual meeting that his greatest skill is avoiding bad luck. Ironically, he says that isn't a skill, it's luck. He discussed how luck played a great role not only in his investing success, but in many other areas in his life, including living well into his 90s. "If you're lucky in life, make sure a bunch of other people are lucky, too.", Buffett said.

CHAPTER 24
OPPORTUNITY COST

Many say stock investing is "mostly mental," but I disagree. Well, maybe it is some mental, but I say that achieving investing success is "mostly being in the right stocks." They call it a *stock* portfolio and *stock* investing for a reason. It is not called the *technical analysis* market or *technical analysis* investing; it is called *stock* investing and the *stock* market, and there is a heavy cost to pay for being in the wrong stocks. I feel that many investors in today's world get so caught up and distracted talking about everything *other* than the stock itself. There are so many distractions on business shows on television, in macroeconomics, and other metrics besides the stock itself. You often hear people say "it's a stock picker's market." That may be true, but the problem is most people are very bad at picking the right stocks. As if stock investing wasn't already hard enough, the regrets you have can invoke even more pain, thinking about one stock versus another you could have bought.

When stocks go down, you buy shares. When stocks go up, you make money. You can't lose, right? But what if the stock doesn't go up, or never gets back to your average buy price? Or it takes a decade to go back up, and in the meantime, there is opportunity cost of other stocks that went up more?

Microsoft stock had a 15% total return from 2000 to 2015, and that is a great and stable company. You might run out of both time and patience to hold Microsoft stock that entire time and not just sell all your shares. You must be aware of the opportunity cost of what you could have been in while Microsoft did nothing for 15 years. Let's discuss this below, as data does not lie.

Let's compare the returns of some very popular billion-dollar companies that almost everyone has heard of to prove my opportunity cost point. The results may surprise you. Let us start with the Coke vs Pepsi debate, which among consumers has been very public and ongoing for decades. People also get attached to one or the other stock too. We will benchmark each stock's return to the S&P 500 Index, in this case Vanguard's (ticker: VOO) Index Fund. We will compare 10 years, from July 2014 thru July 2024. By picking such a long time period, there's no excuse of 'cherry picking' data. I would also like to point out that total returns are with dividends reinvested. Vanguard Index Fund (ticker: VOO), up 267% is the 'benchmark.' The point of this exercise is to examine the indirect price you might have paid choosing the 'wrong' stock, from a total return perspective.

Coca Cola versus Pepsi

Coca Cola stock (ticker: KO) has long been one of Warren Buffett's favorite holdings. I wonder if Warren knows Pepsi (ticker: PEP) has greatly outperformed Coca Cola. What's a few billion dollars lost to Warren Buffett anyway? This also proves you need to pick the *right* sugar when picking your sugar stock to own, as both companies produce a lot of sugary drinks. From the looks of the results here, it appears you shouldn't pick *any* of these two sugar stocks, as the benchmark Index soundly beat both Coke and Pepsi returns.

Coca Cola +105%

Pepsi +145%

VOO Index +267%

Amazon versus Google

For this analysis, let's look at two of the most widely known and popular technology stocks. We learned about the power of Amazon stock compounding in Chapter 7 when we talked about former pro baseball player Alex Rodriguez. Amazon stock has been one of the biggest compounding stocks of all-time, assuming you got into the stock early. Google is one of the most well-known technology stocks and largest companies in the world. Amazon nearly doubled Google's returns, but both clearly beat the Index by a lot.

Amazon +1,074%

Google +545%

VOO Index +267%

MetLife versus Prudential Insurance

We have discussed some of the more popular and exciting stocks in the entire stock market. Now, let's take a short break and discuss two of the more boring stocks out there: MetLife (ticker: MET) and Prudential Insurance (ticker: PRU). They both are very popular and large insurance stocks, and some parts of their businesses compete against each other. Both are considered relatively safe stocks that pay a consistent dividend. These are the chief reasons people own either stock. It is not surprising how close the results are. The results for both are not bad, but well short of the Index returns.

MetLife +116%

Prudential +107%

VOO Index +267%

Texas Roadhouse versus Darden Restaurants

Now, let's discuss one of my favorite things in life to do: eat. To be honest, who really doesn't like food and talking about food. Darden Restaurants (ticker: DRI) seemingly owns every great restaurant, and I've eaten at them all. Darden Restaurants, Inc., together with its subsidiaries, owns and operates full-service restaurants in the United States and Canada. It operates under Olive Garden, Longhorn Steakhouse, The Capital Grille, Seasons 52, and others. Texas Roadhouse (ticker: TXRH) is an American steakhouse chain that specializes in steaks in a

Texan and Southwestern cuisine style. They also are growing and have restaurants in other countries. There is a Texas Roadhouse near where I live. I go there often and I enjoy their food. In our study here, Texas Roadhouse more than doubled Darden's returns, and both beat the Index.

Darden Restaurants +307%

Texas Roadhouse +631%

VOO Index +267%

Just for good measure, since we are talking about food stocks in this section, let's throw Starbucks (ticker: SBUX) into the discussion. Starbucks would be a good benchmark to use against any food stock, since it is very popular and has been around a long time. Starbucks stock is up 127% during that ten-year time period we defined in the beginning of this chapter. Starbucks has clearly greatly underperformed both restaurant stocks, but has quite substantially lagged VOO as well. As disappointing as this may be for you if you own Starbucks stock (I do not own the stock), I do still enjoy going to Starbucks.

What we have learned in this chapter is how to look at opportunity cost. Opportunity cost is defined as the potential forgone profit from a missed opportunity, the result of choosing one alternative over another. The loss of potential gain from other alternatives when one alternative is chosen. Regarding opportunity cost in stock investing, it can either make you very happy or very sad. This depends on how the stock, or whatever asset you own, compares to other stocks you could have owned over the time of ownership. For example, if you were in cash the entire time Nvidia stock went up 1,000% and you didn't own Nvidia, then you may be sad.

CHAPTER 25
KEEP INVESTING AFTER RETIREMENT

Many financial planners will say stocks are indispensable for every investor, young or old, as they are the only asset that can beat inflation over long periods. Based on past returns stocks are more likely than other investments to help your portfolio and keep up with inflation. Stocks give you the possibility of higher returns and thus the possibility of higher future income. A good rule of thumb is to subtract your age from 110 to determine your ideal stock allocation. If you're 40, this means you should theoretically have about 70% of your portfolio in stock investments.

People should continue investing in stocks after retirement, as you may live a lot longer than you anticipated. I can speak firsthand because I have someone in my family who cashed out most of her stocks post-retirement and regrets the decision. My schoolteacher aunt retired in her early sixties. When she did, she took all her money out of the stock market because she was risk averse and afraid of one day losing it. One cannot fault her or pass judgment for thinking that way, but if she had just put a part of her cash savings into a S&P 500 Index fund, she would have had over a million extra dollars today. At the time of her retirement, and even now, she could live off just her pension and Social Security, but did not want to risk her money. Her mother lived to 96 so, genetically speaking, she is likely to live to a similar age, if not longer. Due to advances in medicine people are living longer and longer. Many people are in danger of outliving their money. Personally, I plan on staying invested in some capacity in stocks forever.

One could argue that my aunt risked losing a portion of her money had she invested in stocks in her early sixties. That is true. However, she had a nice pension and Social Security to live on, so she could have easily taken on more risk. Do you realize how much the stock market has risen over the past 20 years that she wasn't invested in the market? I'm not saying that seventy and eighty-year-olds should be day trading on Robinhood. However, even if you just had *some* money in a S&P 500 Index fund over that time you could have done very well. For seniors, a lot of it boils down to the emotions related to investing in the stock market. Some people cannot sleep at night with a large portion of their money in the stock market, and this line of thinking is understandable. Many have the mindset of "more money more problems." There is actually a famous song called "Mo Money Mo Problems."

My aunt can live off her pension and Social Security, but she could have been doing much better if she had remained invested in the stock market, in some capacity. She will be living longer, so she may need additional money down the road that could have been earned in investments.

CHAPTER 26
WHY THE STOCK MARKET MAY KEEP GOING UP

The U.S. stock market has gone up rather dramatically the past ten years. In this chapter, we will examine the reasons why and that it could very well continue its upward trajectory, of course barring a Black Swan event or asteroid hitting Earth. In no particular order, below are potential reasons for growth:

1. **There are simply fewer public companies today than there were decades ago.** The number of publicly listed companies traded on U.S. exchanges has fallen substantially from its peak in 1996. Back then, the number exceeded 8,000 companies. Today, that count has dropped by more than 50% to just 3,700, according to data from the Center for Research in Security Prices (June 9th, 2023). Why? Low interest rates in the 2000s and a boom of capital available with both venture capital and private equity has contributed. A smaller company can now get capital for growth without the pains (and compliance issues) associated with going public. Another possible reason for the decline may be that many companies were simply acquired by others.

A higher rate of M&A activity could very well partly explain the reason behind the shrinkage.

2. **The growth of corporations buying back their own shares has also gained traction.** Every CEO is concerned about their earnings per share, or EPS, since the valuation of their stock is usually tied directly to EPS. Earnings per share is simply earnings divided by the number of shares outstanding. Simple math dictates there are two ways to make EPS increase: increase the numerator (earnings), or decrease the denominator (shares outstanding). Almost every year since 2004 has seen S&P 500 companies spend more on their own share buybacks than on paying dividends to their shareholders. One example of a visible company that has done this often is Apple. At the beginning of 2013, Apple had 26.3 billion shares outstanding. From that point up until today, Apple has consistently repurchased their shares on the open market. Fast forward to today and Apple has around 15 billion shares outstanding. What do you think has happened to Apple stock's share price during that time period? It has gone up a lot. Many companies are not even issuing new shares because they feel it's dilutive to the share price. Buybacks typically rise when earnings rise. This is because as earnings rise, which is currently happening at its fastest pace in nearly two years, cash flow at companies increases. Companies can then use this cash flow to increase dividends paid

to shareholders, increase capital expenditures to invest back in the company, or repurchase stock, and, in turn, return capital to shareholders.

3. **The proliferation of ETFs and index funds and people's retirement plans and IRAs automatic monthly deposits into these has increased.** Hence, there will be more dollars chasing fewer stocks available to purchase. One can assume that certain stock prices of the ones that are included in these indexes may continue to climb.

FINAL THOUGHTS

I'd like to wrap up this chapter with a few thoughts. Unfortunately, inflation can compound in the same way interest earned compounds. Compound inflation has the opposite effect and decreases your purchasing power. Interest *earned* will compound upwards with time. Inflation *suffered* will decrease the value of nominal cash in terms of real purchasing power. At the time of writing, inflation is going down here in the United States, which essentially means the rate of inflation is not going up as much. The problem can be that over the course of years, prices of homes, cars, insurance, etc. became 'permanently inflated.' Investors look for ways to beat this inflation. They go further out on the risk spectrum in search of decent returns because there isn't enough income to be had with the majority of traditional investments. Investors 'chase yield' to try to find an investment that can at least keep pace, or hopefully outpace compound inflation. Investors could collectively push the stock market up because there is no other viable alternative than stocks to keep pace with high inflation. This also gets back to Chapter 15 on Bitcoin. Bitcoin could be that 'escape hatch.' These are all just my thoughts and opinions. You would have to do your own research and draw your own conclusions.

CHAPTER 27
FINANCIAL EDUCATION

Remember in high school when they taught us algebra and what a Venn diagram was but not how the stock market works? Which one do you think will get you wealthy today? Were your parents and grandparents good stock investors and, if so, did they teach you anything about stock investing? My guess would be it is doubtful they were, and didn't teach you much of anything about investing.

Here is a 'real life' example of why financial education is necessary. A recent exchange with my neighbor, who purchased my first stock investing book *Night Trading* in 2022, and it is now mid-2024. I should also note that he works 60 hours a week.

> **Me:** "Have you read my stock investing book yet?" I asked.

> **Him:** "Not yet. I've been too busy to read it. I'll get around to investing one day," he responded.

Would you allow a teenager to drive a car without any driver's education? Unfortunately, we allow our youth and young adults to enter the complex financial world without any basic financial literacy. There are hardly any financial literacy classes in high school. One could call the situation financial *illiteracy*. Currently only 26 U.S. states require high school students to take a financial literacy course in order to graduate. This is actually not as bad as it looks, because the number of states requiring a financial literacy course has been steadily increasing, and one day will hit all 50 states.

Kids are rarely learning about personal finance at home, either. Studies show that parents are reluctant, uncomfortable, and often not qualified to teach financial management to their kids. Personally speaking, I would also add that from my experience most parents I know are completely unequipped to be able to teach their kids how to invest because they themselves are not qualified enough. Hence, this created half the reason for me writing this book. It shocks me how many people I know, some very wealthy, who do not understand the stock market or investing in it at all. In my opinion, you not only need to live your life with a sense of urgency, you should invest with a sense of urgency.

High school seems like the best and most logical place to begin delivering personal finance education to America's youth. The 2008 financial crisis and subsequent large stock market correction clearly showed that poor financial decisions by individuals had negative consequences on our country. There are many studies that show that individuals with higher levels of financial literacy make better personal finance decisions. As a society, we need more training programs that increase the number of financially literate citizens, who will then be able to make better and wiser financial decisions. Reading this book and having quality and experienced financial people like myself "guest teaching" at our high schools and colleges would be a great start. I do not even like to use the word literacy anymore when discussing financial literacy, as it seems like you are saying or assuming someone might be illiterate. I prefer to call it financial education, and I've seen others in this field call it that as well. It sounds better. Maybe one of the reasons we appear to not make much progress on financial literacy, is we've been naming it wrong all these years by attaching the stigma of the closely related word illiteracy.

I feel that achieving the goal of promoting financial education in our high schools and colleges does not necessarily have to cost a fortune. Remember, this book costs much less than taking a family of four to McDonald's for dinner, and I think you can get a lot of "bang for your buck" from it. Most of the work on the road to nationwide financial education requires mostly an investment of people's time. Maybe if more people invested their time and learned stock investing, people like my neighbor could retire earlier and have more time to spend with their kids.

CONCLUSION
THINKING SIMPLE AND COMPLEX

Investing can sometimes boil down to a few key questions: Are you renting or buying? Are you in it for the short or long term? No matter your answers, try to always be invested in the stock market, or whatever investment vehicle you choose. There is an old sports quote that "you miss 100% of the shots you don't take."

Since 1928, the S&P 500 yearly returns, including dividends, have been up approximately 72% and down only 28% of the time. Roughly three out of four years the market is up. I am willing to take those odds. However, anyone investing during a rising bull market can look like a stock-picking genius. You do not have to work as hard to be successful during a bull market. During a bear market, though, you will need to put in the extra time, leaning on the things you have learned in this book.

The stock market is very much like sports – if the deck is stacked in your favor and you have all the star players, you will likely win. If you own all the stocks that are rising in a growing economy in a rising bull market, then it's likely your stock portfolio will do well. One only needs to look what happened to the Patriots football team when Tom Brady left to play for another NFL team. He led his new team to the Super Bowl title in just one year, while the team he left crumbled. The same thing happened when Michael Jordan left the Chicago Bulls – the team was not as successful. Another difficult part about investing *and* professional sports is that no one can predict the unpredictable. You can still have all the best information and the best players but still lose the game and, in the stock market, all your money. A perfect explanation of this from Investopedia: "A black swan is an unpredictable event that is beyond what is normally expected of a situation and has potentially severe consequences. Black swan events are characterized by their extreme rarity, severe impact, and the widespread conclusion that they were obvious in hindsight." Examples would be the Covid-19 pandemic in 2020, or a more extreme case The Great Depression of 1929.

There is an emotional part to investing as well. You occasionally must take calculated risks and go with the hot hand. Ride the wave, and then catch another wave. Think, but do not overthink. Gather as much information as you can, so you can use it to your advantage.

Also, always try to work on building out your network of friends to 'plug yourself in' to hot stock and other investment tips, with all publicly available information. I got some of my best investment ideas and tips from other friends and investors, some of whom knew nothing about stocks or investing. It is much better to have others do all the heavy lifting and investment research. If you are too overwhelmed with the idea of investing entirely on your own, or just do not have the time, then recalibrate and buy only ETFs or index funds. Don't buy individual stocks if you think they're too risky.

Risk is always a factor when discussing stocks and investing. It is about what level of risk you want to take on. If you have a low appetite for risk then you could buy Hershey, which we discussed in Chapter 20, with a beta of only .35. Or, if you feel like taking on more risk, you could buy Tesla stock, which has a much riskier beta of 2.31, at the time of writing. Both are thought of as solid companies, and have provided excellent returns over the years, if you had a long-term mindset. Tesla, however, offers more risk but has provided much greater returns than Hershey.

Some people have never diversified their stock portfolios, and only bought one stock: Tesla. It may sound crazy and very risky to not diversify, but it's true. These investors took modest investments, and turned them into millions with the meteoric rise of Tesla stock. They call themselves TSLA-naires! By the way, Tesla stock has returned over 12,000% since its 2010 IPO through August of 2024. I also know of people that invest in only Tesla stock and Bitcoin. It is spreading out the risk a tiny bit more, but over time they have done very well for themselves by just investing in Tesla and Bitcoin.

There are a few Olympic sports, figure skating comes to mind, that give out style points. In the game of life, however, no one really cares how you became wealthy. I once spoke with a college basketball coach and I told him how amazed I was at high school kids that could dunk a basketball in a game. He looked at me and said, "Yeah, but a dunk still only counts as two points." So true. You need to mentally think about this 'dunk' statement because it pertains a lot to stock investing, and quite frankly life. You don't always need to do something fancy to succeed. Boring may get the job done, and work just fine.

Staying mostly grounded in dividend-paying stocks, and only occasionally venturing out to alternative investments that could pay off big, is also another piece of investment advice if your risk tolerance allows for it. Most of my stock portfolio is grounded in large, solid, proven corporations, many of which pay a dividend. You didn't need to be the first investor in Amazon or Google to become a millionaire. It's fine if you invested in them even after they became established. When you invest in Fortune 500 companies, then you could be exposed to less risk when the stock market inevitably crashes or corrects. In the early 2000s when the dotcom bubble burst, the Internet itself did not burst or disappear. What ended up bursting and crashing were the thousands of unestablished, unprofitable, and speculative companies that many people invested in.

It is also advantageous to have a sense of awareness of the current macroeconomic and investment environment. I try to be aware of projections for inflation, unemployment, and interest rates for the next twelve months, and factor those statistics into my investment decisions accordingly. Also, sometimes you are best served by going with your gut instincts. Looking back at the best investments over my lifetime, some of my most successful ones have been where I didn't listen to what everyone else said, and believed in my own convictions.

A secular market is a market that is driven by forces that could be in place for many years, causing the price of a particular investment or asset class to rise or fall over a long period. In a secular bull market, positive conditions such as low interest rates and strong corporate earnings push stock prices higher. Conversely, in a secular bear market, stock prices move lower. We have been in a bull market since around 2009, as stocks have moved up appreciably since then. The consensus among financial experts is that we will continue to be in this secular bull market until somewhere between 2030-2033.

Experts study past historical patterns of stock markets and use it to project a big picture, macroeconomic view, including demographics, of how this will all play out in the future. Extensive data and research on secular markets is readily available online if you would like to investigate further. Skeptics might ask the question; how could we not have experienced a bear market in the past ten years prior to the pandemic of 2020? They would ask this because that is quite a long time to go without experiencing a bear market in stocks. Technically, a bear market is when stocks fall at least 20% off their highs. Since 2009, we have not had this, but we have had five severe corrections that have effectively functioned as bear markets. This was especially true in 2022, when stocks got hammered; the tech-heavy NASDAQ dropped about 33%, the S&P 500 sank 19%, and the Dow lost about 9%. While one cannot expect the above average returns of the S&P 500 Index to continue for the next ten years, I am still optimistic about the future of the stock market over that upcoming time period.

Across The Street has also talked about how traditional fundamental stock analysis can still work in today's stock market, notably in Chapter 4. I feel the price of this book is more than justified just by what you may have learned in that chapter alone. Most importantly though, as the title of my last book *Night Trading* states, I do not believe it is healthy to obsess over the stock market, or any of your investments during the day. One should be focused on their career, or other aspects of your life during the day, and do the *Night Trading* when everyone else goes to bed.

A few years ago, I remember watching an interview with a billionaire oil investor. He was asked what his secret to success in life was. His immediate response was "having a tolerance for ambiguity." What does that mean exactly, and what does it have to do with investing? I think having a tolerance for ambiguity allows one to deal with uncertain and unpredictable investments that may have great potential. It is important to not dwell if you think you missed the boat on any one particular investment, because other boats will always be out there to jump onboard. For example, there are thousands of stocks available, and you're not going to get a hit on every single one. Try not to have any regrets if you missed out on an investment, just wait for the next boat that's coming to port. Remember, there is a reason the rearview mirror on your car is really small, and the windshield is very big. This means that about 90% of the time in life you should be looking forward.

I am sure most people who invest have a time horizon in their mind for how long they want to own a particular asset. This book, and my last book *Night Trading* explored the question – is the day trader or the long-term stockholder, correct, or is it somewhere in the middle? My opinion is that investing for the long term is the better choice. It doesn't hurt to have the day trader's mentality sometimes, especially when venturing into other alternative assets like Bitcoin, cryptocurrencies, or new technologies. The day trader mindset could even get you out of a bad, or potentially money-losing investment. Be careful, though, because do you really want to be known as the person that bought Amazon when it was $40 and sold it at $45? Remember, at one time even Bitcoin was trading at a penny per coin, and you couldn't give it away to people. Engaging in day trading of stocks and cryptocurrencies may cause you to lose money, but could also *prevent* you from losing *a lot* of money, because in theory, you probably aren't invested long enough to have a huge loss. However, if you are day trading and getting in and out of investments quickly, you may also miss that rocket ship ride up of a potentially great income generator. Warren Buffett summed it up best when he said: "The stock market is designed to transfer money from the active to the patient."

In my opinion, hanging out with wealthy people is very helpful to getting wealthy, and it doesn't always have to cost that much. It only cost me $75 for the ticket to get a seat at dinner to meet star NFL football player Micah Parsons in person. And I spent only $50 in early 2024 to attend a Bitcoin conference in Manhattan where I met famed investor Cathie Wood. At that same conference, I also met and spoke with Mike Novogratz, who is a billionaire and Bitcoin investor. Mike is the founder, CEO and majority shareholder of Galaxy Digital Holdings, a crypto investment firm that trades on the Toronto Stock Exchange. And in August of 2023 I met Jim Cramer on the floor of the NYSE. Meeting Jim Cramer cost me nothing, as I was introduced through a mutual friend. The point of all this is there are wealthy people all around you. And if you don't personally know any, maybe you just aren't looking hard enough to find them. What if you live in a remote part of Wyoming, though, and you can't find any wealthy people or get to the New York Stock Exchange in Manhattan? Try to connect with wealthy people online. Or, just buy my book and read it, which you obviously are right now.

One of the most important pieces of advice I would give is to have fun in life, and try not to have stock investing consume your entire life. I have yet to see someone's headstone that read: "They Were A Great Stock Investor". They also don't give out Nobel prizes to 'Best Stock Investor.'

I should not even be alive right now. It may be morbid to say that, but had I not followed this one piece of simple advice my parents and grandparents told me as a child, I would not be here now: "Look both ways before crossing the street." A few months ago, I came within one second of dying in my car as another car ran a red light at an intersection I was stopped at. The other car was traveling at about 50 miles per hour, and if I had gone when the light turned green, I'd a been done. The only thing that saved me was listening to the above quote. Risk management, I guess. Life can change very quickly, in both good and bad ways. Sometimes in the stock market, risk management and being cautious will save you. The other thing that might have come into play here in my near-death experience is focusing. I discussed focus in detail in Chapter 5, and how important it is to focus and not get distracted. If I had been talking to someone while driving, or playing with my car radio, then the outcome would have been very bad. This all harkens back to what I prior said about not only living life with a sense of urgency, but also investing in the stock market with a sense of urgency.

One important lesson I have learned over the years is that you need a part of your brain to think in a complex way, and a part that has plain common sense when investing. If you bought Google (ticker: GOOG) stock five years ago and held it, it's up 235%. That 235% return is actually a 3.35x return on your original investment. So, for example, a $1 million investment in Google stock would have ended you up with $3.35 million in total (netting you around $2.35 million before taxes). Not a bad risk/return investment in only five years. Keep in mind, the beta of Google stock is right around 1.0, the same as the S&P 500 Index. You also wouldn't have needed to pay anybody to tell you to just buy and hold Google stock for five years, as you probably could have figured this out by yourself.

Guess what though, if you love Apple (many people do) over Android, you could have just bought Apple stock instead. Apple stock greatly outperformed Google the past five years, gaining approximately 470%. As we learned back in Chapter 11, Apple stock makes up 43% of Warren Buffett's portfolio. I prior said in this book that, in my opinion: "Stock investing isn't mostly mental – it's mostly being in the right stocks." Being in Google or Apple stock proved this concept. You would have to do your own research and thinking, though, on this topic, and there is no guarantee that Google or Apple stock will give you the same great returns in the next five years. What you could also do is compare real estate as an investment to Google or Apple stock over that 5-year time period. While real estate did appreciate a lot, I highly doubt you could have achieved the same or better return flipping houses than the appreciation of Google and Apple stock. Your house would have had to appreciate three to five times its value in just five years.

If you didn't want to invest in technology at all, you could have done what I did and invest in grocery store stock Sprouts Farmers Market (ticker: SFM), which was discussed in detail in Chapter 22. Sprouts has a beta of only .55. My Sprouts investment started with my gut instinct, and thinking simple. I had been eating mostly organic foods myself for the last several decades. I thought it might be a good idea to invest in the stock of a company centered around eating healthy, natural, and organic foods. This should make you recall the 'buy what you know' chapter.

Sometimes, when I think about a stock, I will toss stock charts and all kinds of other crazy analysis out the window, and just pull up a United States map. Sprouts, for example, is one of the best performing stocks the past five years (at time of writing) – up a whopping 428%. Total addressable market (TAM) demonstrates the entire revenue opportunity that exists within a market for a product or service. Here is a map of Sprouts' current stores in the U.S. As you can clearly see, their current footprint in the U.S. is only about half of the total states. So, their TAM and growth opportunities are both huge. Yes, of course they have competition, but Sprouts seems to have figured out the formula to success, and just needs to replicate it throughout the entire U.S. Sprouts may end up being one of my best stock investments ever.

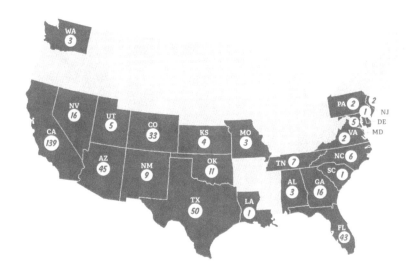

You can pull up a country map of a stock you own or are looking to buy. If they have physical stores, you can look at the company's annual report for a map like I just did and visually see their current footprint. Ask yourself: What is their TAM, and do they have a lot of room to expand? Are there opportunities to expand internationally?

At the end of the day, you might decide that Google or Apple stock, or even Sprouts Farmers Market is too risky for your tastes. That is fine, because as we learned in Chapter 9, you can invest in an S&P 500 Index fund and possibly do well. The Vanguard S&P 500 Index ETF (ticker: VOO) has returned 107% the past five years. So, if you had simply just invested in this you would have doubled your money. I think most would be happy with that return.

One final thought, and maybe the most important thing I have learned about stock investing, and investing in general, is to 'think incrementally.' Do not think too big, and have patience. I'm sure Warren Buffett didn't sit down in 1950 and say to himself he was eventually going to make $100 billion dollars. He probably was sitting where you are right now, wondering where he should start. You're lucky – you have this book to guide you.

Dave Gretta holds an MBA in Financial Management from Pace University in Manhattan and has 30 years of investing experience spanning stocks, bonds, gold, REITs, and cryptocurrencies. Dave is currently an information technology and database professional. Dave worked for many years literally 'across the street' from Wall Street in lower Manhattan as a financial systems analyst and an accountant. His stock investment approach is one that combines fundamental analysis with the ability to adapt to new and changing investment trends while being strongly grounded in the teachings of Warren Buffett, Peter Lynch, and John Bogle. Technical stock analysis and using, analyzing, and interpreting stock charts also factors into Dave's investment decisions. Dave also guest teaches at his boys' high school a class called Stock Market Investing for Beginners. Dave also volunteers his time coaching youth basketball.

Please visit the *Across The Street From Wall Street* book website at www.nighttradingbook.com to leave the author a comment. This website also has a link to Dave's prior book *Night Trading*.